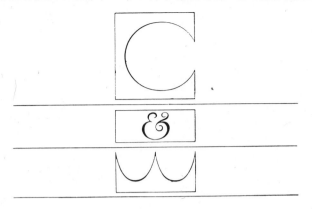

TRAGEDY

Serious Drama in relation to Aristotle's Poetics

F. L. LUCAS

BARNES & NOBLE BOOKS
TOTOWA, NEW JERSEY

First published in the United States 1981
by Barnes & Noble Books
81 Adams Drive
Totowa, New Jersey, 07512

ISBN 0–389–20141–3

Printed in Great Britain

To
CLIVE BELL

Ces sortes de spéculations ne donnent point de génie à ceux qui en manquent; elles n'aident pas beaucoup à ceux qui en ont, et le plus souvent les gens de génie sont incapables d'être aidés par les spéculations. A quoi donc sont-elles bonnes? A faire remonter jusqu'aux premières idées du beau quelques gens qui aiment le raisonnement, et qui se plaisent à réduire sous l'empire de la philosophie les choses qui en paroissent le plus indépendantes, et que l'on croit communément abandonnées à la bizarrerie des goûts.—FONTENELLE

Des théories discutées en si bonne compagnie excitaient nos imaginations à nous représenter vivement les divins ouvrages de sculpture ou de musique dont nous discutions. Voilà, ce me semble, le mécanisme par l'effet duquel les théories sont si agréables aux dilettanti et si importunes aux artistes... Canova était trop bon et trop heureux pour nous haïr; je pense seulement que souvent il ne nous écoutait pas.—STENDHAL

Contents

Preface

WHEN this small book was written in 1927, it was with no expectation that it would remain in demand for thirty years. But since the unexpected has happened, it seemed now desirable to bring it more up to date, and to make some additions (amounting to about fifty per cent of the original volume) which I hope may serve both the general reader and the student of drama.

I am most grateful for valuable suggestions and comments to Professor D. L. Page and Mr. D. W. Lucas.

1

ARISTOTLE

THERE is something Roman about Aristotle. He has not soared into immortality with the bright grace of the Greek; he has conquered it, province by province, with the resolution, the monumental strength, the practical good sense of Rome. Long after the ancient world had fallen into ruin, the ways his thought had paved still guided the medieval mind amid the thickets of its theology; just as the Roman roads ran on across the wasted lands where the eagles had yielded place to the raven and the crow. And as, even to-day, when we whirl along our highways, we still cannot go far without following or crossing some undeviating vestige of the march of Rome, so beneath many lines of modern thought endure the foundations laid by the master of Alexander the Great. This is particularly true of the criticism of Tragedy. There are places where Aristotle's foundations have given way, places where he leads us wrong; but even where he leads us wrong, he leads us straight. Here is none of that twisting and wriggling and rambling too common in modern criticism. One knows always that Aristotle means something, though it may be wrong; as one knows with Johnson, and with the tribes of would-be Coleridges one does not know. Aristotle's curt comments on the Attic drama may seem dry enough in comparison with the mixture of incense-smoke and holy water now sometimes supposed to aid appreciation of a play of Shakespeare; but better be dry than rotten.

If, then, it is asked by some modernist whether it is really necessary at this time of day to hark back to the dramatic opinions of a Greek philosopher in the fourth century B.C., the answer is not so much that Tragedy, both the word and the thing, is Greek by origin—for we are concerned with what Tragedy has become, not merely with what it was; nor that the experience of twenty-three centuries has proved Aristotle infallible—for it has not. The truth is that we should go back to Aristotle not so much for the right answers as for the right questions. To ask them is the first step towards truth—as when Newton asked why apples fall; and to ask them was one of the greatest gifts of Greece. Greek art has had its due of praise; but this other greatness of theirs is less often trumpeted. Other races have fashioned into art and story dreams as lovely; but it is from the Greek that Europe has learnt, so far as it has learnt, to question as well as to dream, to take nothing on earth, or in heaven, for granted—that unfaith, in a word, which has also removed mountains. The annals of Israel are filled with rebellions of the Chosen People against Jehovah; but it never occurs to them to abandon one deity except in exchange for another, or to ask whether it was after all reasonable to suppose that creation began with a man and a woman, a

serpent and an apple. And so with the other ancient
nations that we know. They loved, as most men do
still, certainty better than truth. Greece too had its
myths and its theology; but it is as though such
things had never been, when one day in the sixth
century B.C. Thales of Miletus in Ionia quietly asks,
"Of what is the Universe composed?" and answers,
"Of water." He had divined the underlying homo-
geneousness of matter. His particular answer is, as it
happens, false; we are looking for the true one still;
but the great thing is that man has begun the quest
with his intellect in place of his fantasy. As with
Thales and his successors, so with the eternal, ironic
questioning of Socrates; and so with Aristotle. His
answers, too, we shall again and again find wanting:
much comes to light in twenty-three centuries, dark
as many of them have been; but there is to this day
no better starting point for the study of serious
drama than the *Poetics*—regarded as a *questionnaire*.
If this brief treatise became for centuries after the
Renaissance a millstone round the neck of dramatists, that is because the Greek philosopher was not
studied in the Greek spirit of sceptical inquiry, but
rather as if he had been a Hebrew prophet verbally
inspired. This is no exaggeration of the amazing
authority once enjoyed by Aristotle's philosophy as a
whole. When, for instance, an Italian commentator
found a seeming inconsistency between Aristotle and
the Bible, to Dacier that was a *reductio ad absurdum*
in itself. "As if," he cried, "Divinity and the Holy
Scripture *could* be contrary to the sentiments of

Nature on which Aristotle founds his judgments!"
Even to the temperate Lessing the *Poetics* appeared
"as infallible as the elements of Euclid"; and there
have been more modern critics to whom these pages
remained almost sacred still. Naturally the paradox
of treating a Greek philosopher as another Moses,
and bringing the infallibilities of meaner minds into
that free Greek world of thought, brought equally
violent revolts. Aristotle has been "the master of
those who know" only for those who know also what
"master" means, and that a teacher is not a tyrant.[1]
The reaction against medieval scholasticism involved
also the Greek philosopher it had honoured. Ramus
maintained the thesis that "all Aristotle said was
false"; Bacon called him "the worst of sophists, be-
mused with futile subtlety, the poor plaything of
verbiage"[2]; Hobbes (according to Aubrey) averred
"that Aristotle was the worst Teacher that ever was,
the worst Politician and Ethick—a Countrey-fellow
that could live in the World would be as good"
(though he owned the *Rhetoric* and the *Discourse of
Animals* to be "rare"). To-day idolatry and denigra-
tion alike have died away. But the *Poetics*, ill-written,
incomplete lecture-notes as they are, provide even

[1] Cf. the case of the Abbé d'Aubignac who composed a bad
tragedy in complete conformity with all the precepts of Aristotle.
"I am grateful to M. d'Aubignac," said M. le Prince, "for having
followed so faithfully the rules of Aristotle; but I cannot forgive the
rules of Aristotle for making M. d'Aubignac write such a bad
tragedy." (Saint-Evremond.)

[2] "Pessimus sophista, inutili subtilitate attonitus, verborum vile
ludibrium."

now the basis for an inquiry into the nature of drama. Those few pages ask, if they do not answer, much that we need to know.

Aristotle (384-322 B.C.) was born at Stagīrus (later Stagīra) in Chalcidice, N.W. of Mount Athos. He was the son of Nicomachus, court-physician to Amyntas II of Macedon; and so, probably, became early acquainted with the king's youngest son and future successor, Philip, who was one day to make Aristotle tutor to *his* heir, Alexander the Great.

At seventeen, in 368-7, Aristotle began the first phase of his career—a twenty years' residence in Athens as a member of Plato's Academy. When Plato died (348-7), he was succeeded as head of the Academy by his nephew Speusippus—not, it appears, a very intelligent person. (He thought pleasure an evil, as well as pain; though himself accused of voluptuous self-indulgence. That, however, may be merely philosophic scandal.) At all events Aristotle withdrew to Assos (near Troy and the Hellespont), where Hermeias, lord of Assos and Atarneus, had gathered a circle of Platonists.

But already Persia and the Macedon that was to destroy her eyed each other with distrust. The Persians suspected Hermeias of intriguing with Philip of Macedon; treacherously kidnapped him; carried him to Susa; vainly tried to extract confession by torture; and finally crucified him (342-1). In his memory Aristotle, whose wife Pythias was the dead man's niece and adopted daughter, wrote a poem (still extant) praising Virtue and him who had served her, heroic to the last, like Heracles and the Heavenly Twins, like Ajax and Achilles. It seems to have been daily sung at the common table of Aristotle and his school.

Meanwhile, after three years in Lesbos, busy with biology, in 343-2 Aristotle had been invited by King Philip to his capital of Pella, as tutor to Alexander, then thirteen or fourteen; mainly, it seems, in political science and in literature (especially Homer). For Aristotle refused to follow the puritanical ban of his master, Plato, on poetry in education.

But, despite the presence of philosophy, the court of Pella remained barbarous and sinister as the courts of Mycenae or Elsinore. To marry a new bride, Philip put away his Queen, Olympias; in 336 she had him murdered, and her son Alexander came to the throne. After an absence of some twelve years, Aristotle returned (335-4) to the quiet of Athens. Some twelve years more were left him.

No doubt Athenian patriots like Demosthenes may have knit their brows at this alien, the hereditary friend of that Macedonian monarchy which had crushed Greek freedom at Chaeronea (338); friend, too, of Antipater, left regent of Macedon while Alexander stormed through Asia; and foe to extreme democracy, as to all extremes. But Aristotle was a self-possessed character. On hearing that one had abused him, "Let him even beat me," was his traditional reply, "provided I am not there." And Athens, though broken, was still the intellectual capital of

Hellas, "the eye of Greece". There Aristotle now founded his own school, the Lyceum (to endure over eight centuries, into the days of Justinian), in a grove of Apollo Lyceius south of Lycabettus, and not far from the present British School. Its buildings included a covered walk or walks (*peripatos*—whence the name "Peripatetics"), museum, and library. More and more his mind seems to have turned to scientific study of concrete realities; as if he had taken to heart the old Chinese saying—"I spent a whole day meditating—I should have done better to learn; I stood on tiptoe for a good view—better had I climbed a hill." And so research was now organized by him on an encyclopedic scale—in politics (for example, constitutional studies of 158 Greek states), history, literature, natural science and biology (where he won the lasting admiration of Darwin). Aristotle had become what Dante calls him—"the Master of those who *know*".[1]

But his last years were not unshadowed. His wife had died; Alexander, though he had sent his old tutor biological data from his conquests, deteriorated with success, saw fit to become a god, ignored (rightly or wrongly) Aristotle's advice to treat his Greek subjects on a higher footing than Orientals, and put to death Aristotle's nephew, the tactless Callisthenes. Lastly, when Alexander himself expired at Babylon (323), Athens leapt to arms against the Macedonians; and, as part of the campaign, Aristotle

[1] Cf. the medieval belief that he drowned himself in the Euripus off Chalcis because he could not fathom the mystery of its ebb and flow.

was accused of impiety, largely for the praises lavished in his poem, years ago, on his dead father-in-law Hermeias. To save the Athenians, as he put it, "from sinning against philosophy a second time",[1] the old philosopher withdrew to Chalcis in Euboea, where he died next year (322), aged sixty-three. We still have the will in which he provided with careful considerateness for his family and slaves, in particular for his mistress Herpyllis and his son by her; with his own ashes were to be laid, as she had wished, those of his dead wife Pythias.

His output had been prodigious. But his published works, largely dialogues once admired for their "golden" style, are lost. The manuscripts of his extant treatises, more in the nature of lecture-memoranda, nearly suffered the same fate. For two centuries they seem to have lain, mouldering and moth-eaten, at Scepsis in the Troad, where the family of one of his disciples had hidden them in a cellar from the book-grabbing Kings of Pergamum. About 100 B.C. they were brought to light and sold; in 84 carried off by Sulla, when he took Athens; and re-edited in Rome.[2]

It is easy to picture Aristotle as an encyclopedic

---

[1] Referring, of course, to the execution of Socrates (399). But "second time" is understatement; Athens had prosecuted also Anaxagoras, Diagoras, and perhaps Protagoras.

[2] The Second Book of the *Poetics* (on Comedy) seems to have been lost before the seventh century A.D., about which time our treatise was translated into Syriac, whence it passed about A.D. 1000 into Arabic. The Syriac has perished in its turn, but for a fragment: the Arabic survives, as well as various Greek MSS., of which the

dryasdust—a ponderous, though subtle, elephant, picking up innumerable pins. "Whatever he touched," I once heard a Platonist professor exclaim, "he petrified." Unhappy students may complain that he dissects tragedy as drily as a biologist a sea-urchin, and writes of poetry with utter prosiness—as Maupertuis was said to write of happiness in a tone to make one weep. Vain to expect much mutual sympathy between "tender-minded" Platonists and "tough-minded" Aristotelians.

Yet Aristotle needs to be judged with some of his own moderation. His toughness should not be exaggerated. He never wholly threw off the influence of his old master, Plato. Tradition portrays a somewhat unexpected figure—bald and thin-legged, but dapper in dress, with rings on his fingers and in his expression a mocking irony.[1] It is hard to estimate a writer from unpolished and unpublished lecture-notes; and if the *Poetics* seems prosy, the poem on the dead Hermeias reveals a strength of feeling we should not have guessed.[2]

There is good sense in the comment on him of a poet—Gray: "Then he has a dry Conciseness, that

oldest dates from the tenth or eleventh century. A Latin translation was published in 1498; the first Greek text in 1508.

For its influence since then, see Lane Cooper, *The Poetics of Aristotle* (1924).

[1] Cf. his reported reply to a bore asking "Have I bored you?"— "No, I did not listen"; and his definition of hope—"A waking dream."

[2] Cf. his recorded habit of saying (as David might have, remembering Jonathan, or Montaigne, remembering La Boétie): "Whoever has friends, has no *friend*."

makes one imagine one is perusing a Table of Contents rather than a Book: it tasts for all the World like chop'd Hay, or rather like chop'd Logick; for he has a violent Affection to that Art, being in some Sort his own Invention; so that he often loses himself in little trifleing Distinctions & verbal Niceties, & what is worse leaves you to extricate yourself as you can. thirdly he has suffer'd vastly by the Transcribblers, as all Authors of great Brevity necessarily must. fourthly and lastly he has abundance of fine uncommon Things, wch make him well worth the Pains he gives one" (to Wharton, Sept. 1746).[1]

It remains sufficiently astonishing that this brief dramatic treatise, written in ignorance of all drama but that produced in one tiny corner of the earth's surface during one tiny span of the world's history,[2] should still, twenty-three centuries later, be read from California to Calcutta. Has its profundity been overpraised? Possibly. But it is terse[3]; it is honest; it shows a very keen eye for vital points. To some it may recall a Greek mountaintop in the storms of a Greek spring—grey stones, dead prickles, but a keen and piercing air—and at moments, when the mists open, what far glimpses across the dramatic world!

[1] *Correspondence* (ed. Toynbee and Whibley), I. 241.

[2] It is true, Greek drama was extremely prolific—the names are still known of 141 tragic poets and of 387 tragedies. All the same the field open to Aristotle was very different from the vast diversity of world-drama.

[3] Some 10,000 words; it is enough to contrast Castelvetro's *Poetica d' Aristotele vulgarizzata et sposta* of 1570—a great, close-printed volume over fifteen times as long. The second edition of 1576 even doubled this unconscionable bulk.

II

THE DEFINITION OF TRAGEDY

IT is not the purpose of this book to follow the text of Aristotle paragraph by paragraph (for a summary, see Appendix). Commentaries abound. For the general reader or the student of drama, a good deal of the *Poetics* is now dead: its still living value lies in the crucial problems it raises—such as Mimesis, Catharsis, Plot, Character, Style, Unity, Tragic Irony—passages where single sentences have given rise to whole volumes.

But first one must disentangle the Aristotelian and modern senses of "Poetry" (chapter i) and "Tragedy" (chapter vi), which have caused much tedious confusion.

In Greek, *poietes* (from *poiein*, "to make") means—

    (1) a "maker" of anything;
    (2) one who "makes" verses on any subject;
    (3) one who "makes *up*" creative literature in verse (cf. medieval English "maker", and French *trouvère*, *troubadour*).

Aristotle dislikes meaning (2), and prefers (3). He rejects, for example, the claim of Empedocles to be a poet (though praising his style elsewhere), because he wrote merely didactic verse, on philosophy. For Aristotle, poetry must be verse literature that reflects life in creative fiction. I suppose he would similarly have rejected Hesiod, or Lucretius, or Virgil's *Georgics*. This seems to me narrow.[1] But the main thing is to grasp what he meant.[2]

In medieval French and English there persisted a similar sense of "poetry" as invention—the term even covered prose fiction as well.

In modern English the opportunity for muddle continues; and critics have made the most of it. "Poet" means—

(1) one who makes verses;

(2) one who makes fine and moving verses (as opposed to a poetaster);

(3) one who moves our imaginations, even in prose, as a fine poet does (e.g. one can say Sir Thomas Browne is a great poet).

Indeed, by metaphor, "poetry" can even be extended to the power of things not literary at all to

[1] It is curious to contrast Faguet's judgment on Buffon (who did not even write, like Empedocles, in verse)—"le plus grand poète du XVIIIme siècle". In modern eyes, the true poet is often not so much (as for Aristotle) one who writes creative fictions, as one who possesses a certain imaginative power of seeing and feeling poetically life's harsh or prosaic-seeming facts—as if Nature herself were a poet, and the world a riddling poem. So with Hardy, for whom it was a tragic poem.

[2] As it happened, almost all Greek imaginative literature down to Aristotle's day was actually in verse; apart from a few exceptions like the mimes of Sophron or the dialogues of Plato, which Aristotle said were *between* poetry and prose. For, on the one hand, they were lifelike fictions; on the other, they were not in verse. (Was it in Aristotle's mind that his old master, condemning in his dialogues artistic representation, was in writing those very dialogues guilty of it himself? Possibly.)

stir us as does the poet in sense (2)—thus we speak of the "poetry" of moonlight or of spring. (Cf. Lytton Strachey, on Bacon, "It is probably always disastrous not to be a poet. His imagination, with all its magnificence, was insufficient"; and Alfred de Vigny—"Tout homme qui n'a pas de poésie dans le coeur ne sera pas grand.")

Here is a multitude of meanings. Which is the "right" one? All. (For they are all established by usage.) As well squabble about the "right" meaning of "box". There are dozens. The only thing that matters is not to muddle them. The wranglings of centuries whether "poetry" need or need not be in verse, and so forth, are a depressing waste of words. Critics debate which of the verbal thimbles really has the magic pea under it—when there are quite good peas under all.

In practice, Aristotle's *Poetics* is concerned with serious drama (the Greek *tragoidia* need not end unhappily) and, rather perfunctorily, with epic. A lost second book appears to have handled satire and comedy (which paint men, on the contrary, as meaner, not finer, than they ordinarily are). There is no sign that Aristotle discussed elegy or lyric. (This will seem odd; for latterly lyric has tended to become the main, and indeed almost the only, kind of verse to survive.) Why? I do not know. Suggested explanations seem thin. But in any case the *Poetics* is incomplete; and we have lost also another work of Aristotle's, a dialogue in three books *On the Poets*.

Next, the famous definition of Tragedy (vi). There

could be no better example of Aristotle's useful power of provoking disagreement. "Tragedy," he says, "is a representation of an action, which is serious, complete in itself, and of a certain length; it is expressed in speech made beautiful in different ways in different parts of the play[1]; it is acted, not narrated; and by exciting pity and fear it gives a healthy relief to such emotions." Thus Aristotle states in due logical order, first, what tragedy is and represents; secondly, the form it employs; thirdly, the manner in which it is communicated; and, lastly, the function it fulfils. At the outset it must be repeated that, for the Greeks, *tragoidia* need not end in disaster. It must include scenes of pain and sorrow, but it need not close with one; though it usually did.[2] The essence of "tragedy" was that it handled serious actions of serious characters, whereas comedy dealt grotesquely with the grotesque. So essential was this idea of noble seriousness that Plato even extends *tragoidia* to cover non-dramatic poetry like Homer's (whose *Odyssey* also ends happily).

In the Middle Ages "tragedy" curiously changed meaning. Its connection with the stage was forgotten (cf. Plato's extension of the term to epic). By the

[1] This refers to the differences in metre and dialect between the Choric Odes and the Dialogue of Greek Tragedy.

[2] Aristotle (xiii. 6) prefers an unhappy ending; but seems to contradict himself (xiv. 9) by also preferring the type of conclusion where the truth comes to light *before* the irreparable deed is done (e.g. Iphigeneia, about to sacrifice her own brother, finds out who he is, just in time). Perhaps he felt the first to be more deeply moving; the second more satisfying to our humane sympathies.

seventh century Horace, Persius, Juvenal were "tragedians"; in Byzantine Greek τραγῳδία, like the Modern Greek τραγούδι, signified simply "song". But gradually the unhappy ending became essential. For Chaucer, "tragedy" is "a dite of a prosperite for a tyme, that endeth in wrecchidnesse"; like his own *Troilus and Criseyde*, or the dismal episodes with which his Monk annoyed the Pilgrims. Conversely the *Divina Commedia* could earn its name by ending in Paradise. According to Dante an unhappy tale was called a "tragedy" or "goat-song"[1] because goats are noisome; according to his still more ingenious commentator da Buti, because a he-goat, proudly horned and bearded before, is bare and squalid behind.

At the Renaissance the word's connection with drama revived; but its association with a sad ending has remained.[2] Thus "tragedy" has had three meanings—

(1) ancient—serious drama;

(2) medieval—a story with unhappy close;

(3) modern—a drama with unhappy close (disastrous enough for us to feel it "tragic").[3]

---

[1] The real source of the term is still disputed—whether it was that a goat was sacrificed, or a goat was the prize, or the original choric dancers dressed in goatskins, or like goats.

[2] For Castelvetro, however (1505-71), "tragedy" could still have a happy dénouement.

[3] Some would insist on a narrower sense—that the "tragic" must contain also a cosmic sense of the problem of evil, the mystery of the cruelty of things; as in *Agamemnon* or *Hamlet* or *The Dynasts*.

What matters is to remember that Aristotle is really discussing, not what we call "tragedy", but what we call "serious drama".

However, this difference once recognized, his definition may seem simple enough. Yet few sentences in literature, outside theology, have contained a fiercer hornets' nest of controversies.

"Tragedy is a representation, an imitation, of an action" (μίμησις πράξεως). The phrase disappears beneath a crowd of struggling aestheticians; for how far, and in what sense, should Art "imitate" life? It is safer to keep to the Greek word *mimesis*—though *that* is confused enough. *Mimesis* (whence our "mime", "mimic") covers both *representation* of objects with a realism so photographic that, says Plato (*Republic*, 598c), "children or simple folk may be taken in", and, at the opposite extreme, *reproduction* of emotional states by means so far from realistic that Aristotle can even call music "the *most* mimetic of the arts" (*Politics*, viii. 5. 1340A; cf. Plato, *Rep.* 399A, *Laws*, 668A). It also includes the representation that idealizes and the representation that caricatures. A difficult word. Neither Plato nor Aristotle seems to me adequately to disentangle its ambiguities.

Its essence is the artificial reproduction of things in real life—recreation by re-creation.

But (*A*) one can reproduce the *sense-impressions* of real life. (1) The medium used for this may be exactly similar. If you catch a person's likeness in a mirror, or have an effective waxwork made of him (as Duke Ferdinand did with the Duchess of Malfi's husband and children), the light-waves produced are exactly similar. When Plutarch's Parmeno "counterfeited passing well the grunting of an hogge", or the youthful Boswell mooed like a cow at Drury Lane, the sound-waves produced were exactly similar. Or (2) the medium may be widely different. For instance, one may paint in words. When Macbeth exclaims—

> Light thickens, and the Crow
> Makes Wing to th' Rookie Wood,

he may rouse our imaginations to a vivider vision of sinister twilight than could be induced by the most realistic scene-painting and stage-lighting, even aided by an electric crow. As La Fontaine's pigeon put it—

> Mon voyage dépeint
> Vous sera d'un plaisir extrême.
> Je dirai: J'étois là; telle chose m'advint:
> *Vous y croirez être vous-même.*

And of course in this *mimesis* of sense-impressions there are many intermediate degrees of realism. A bronze statue may exactly reproduce shape, but not colour. A painting may exactly reproduce colour and outline, but remains only two-dimensional, and incomprehensible to dogs.

But (*B*) *mimesis* can also denote the reproduction in us, not merely of the sensory impressions, but of

27

the *emotions* of real life.[1] As when Euripides made even the tyrant Alexander of Pherae sorrow with and for the sorrows of Hecuba. (This infectious transference of emotion is, for Tolstoy, the essence of all Art.)

(1) It may do this by means of realistic sensory impressions.

> Just as she was, the painter has caught Theódote.
> Would he had failed!—and let us forget our misery.
>
> (JULIANUS, *Prefect of Egypt*)

Or (2) emotions like those of real life may be *reproduced* in us by means of sensory impressions quite different. Certain music made Boswell long to rush into the thick of the battle. ("Sir," said Johnson, "I should never hear it, if it made me such a fool.") Now this music cannot have looked like a battle; it need not have sounded like one. Similarly in the most erotic melodies there is little likeness between the embrace of lovers and the vibrations of catgut. These mysterious effects of music may, I suppose, depend partly on direct nervous reactions, partly on obscure and largely unconscious associations—just as Pavlov made his dogs' mouths water by whistles not in the least like dog-biscuits. But whatever the cause, it was this unequalled power to reproduce in men emotional states like those of real life that made Aristotle call music "the most mimetic of the arts".[2]

---

[1] L. J. Potts compares Wordsworth's "emotion recollected in tranquillity" (*Aristotle on the Art of Fiction*, 67).

[2] This is not the place to discuss whether we also have *aesthetic* emotions quite unlike those of ordinary life.

Clearly, however, the unfortunate word *mimesis*, strained to cover such a vast diversity of effects, from waxworks to Beethoven, becomes sadly overworked. It breaks down. It grows confused and confusing—a haze and a maze. It traps even Aristotle into seeming self-contradiction (contrast, on epic *mimesis*, iii. 1 and xxiv. 7).

Still one may draw certain conclusions. Since in dramatic art the *mimesis* that reproduces life's emotions is more important than the *mimesis* that reproduces life's sense-impressions—the first is a main end, the second only a means to it[1]—scenic effects should be kept strictly subordinate. As Aristotle puts it (vi. 19), the spectacular element concerns the property-man rather than the poet. And yet scenic realism has often become the bane of drama—not, indeed, in Greece, where it was rudimentary—but in Rome and in the last three centuries. For the death of Marmontel's Cléopâtre, Vaucanson (1709-82) invented a marvellous mechanical asp, which hissed —and the audience was completely distracted by it. Only the more foolish type of public wants live rabbits in *A Midsummer Night's Dream*. The cinema could now cater better for the eighteenth-century lady (*The World*, 1753) who damned the pantomime of the genii because "the brick-kiln was horridly executed and did not smell at all like one". It seems better to rely more on the imagination: it is more

---

[1] And, in excess, a dangerous means. Cf. Diderot's young painter who, before touching his canvas, used to kneel and pray: "Mon Dieu, délivrez-moi du modèle".

important to communicate emotions and ideas.[1] Most of us sympathize with the Spartan who, invited to hear a man counterfeit the nightingale, replied that he would rather hear a real one. Keats managed nightingales better. On the other hand, that moderate man Aristotle might also have pointed out that there is a happy mean between too much realism and too little. Few, for instance, will feel nostalgic at the idea of Quin as Othello in white wig and gloves. It would be harder still to adjust oneself to the dramatic conventions of old China where an official with a white face was thereby known to be good, and one with a red face, bad; where 5000 soldiers were indicated by five banners, a mountain by chairs and tables, water by a flag with a fish on it; and where the scene-shifters were deemed invisible because dressed in black. No doubt one would get used to it; but I do not much want to. However, enough has been said to suggest that there is more involved in the simple-seeming term *mimesis* than might at first sight appear.[2]

"Tragedy," to return to Aristotle's definition, "is a representation of *an action*." Again, how simple! But stay, what exactly constitutes "action"? How much should there be? We remember the differing definitions by which later critics have sought more

[1] Cf. Han Fei Tzu (d. 233 B.C.): "A man spent three years in carving a leaf out of ivory, of such elegant and detailed workmanship that it would lie undetected among a heap of real leaves. But Lieh Tzu said, 'If God Almighty spent three years over every leaf, the trees would be badly off for foliage.'"

[2] See also pp. 162-8.

precision, Brunetière's insistence on "conflict" as the one essential, Archer's on "crisis". We see looming in the future those revolts against the tyranny of mere action, Maeterlinck's Static Drama, Shaw's Discussion Play. And we come to realize how surely and steadily during the centuries between Marlowe and Chekhov the "action" of Tragedy has passed from outside the characters to within them, from the boards to the theatre of the soul, so that at last the whole frontier between action and passion tends to fade away.

"An action that is *serious*"—the Greek word (σπουδαίας) means "that matters", "that is worth troubling about".[1] Here too lurks an ancient quarrel —what *is* in fact "serious" enough for the dignity of tragedy? We hear again the angry invectives of Aristophanes denouncing Euripides for bringing beggars and lovers on the stage of Dionysus; Sidney's strictures on the indecorum "in majestical matters" of that popular drama from which Shakespeare was to spring; the outcries of Racine's enemies at his indecency in making an Emperor hide behind a curtain, or calling a dog a dog in tragedy;

[1] H. House (*Poetics*, 82-3) argues that σπουδαίας means "morally good", on the ground that this is the general usage in Aristotle's *Poetics* and *Ethics*. He has overlooked such passages as *Poetics*, iv. 9: "Just as Homer was supremely a poet on *serious* themes (σπουδαία) . . . so too he first outlined the forms of *comedy*" (cf. σπουδάζεσθαι in v. 2). σπουδαῖος, σπουδάζειν are constantly used in Greek of what has gravity and seriousness (like tragedy), as contrasted with what has levity and playfulness (like comedy). To bring out the full force of the word here, one could render "nobly serious" (cf. Matthew Arnold's "high seriousness").

31

the scandal of the French theatre at the use of the prosaic word "mouchoir" in Vigny's *More de Venise*; the invincible disgust of Coleridge and Sarcey at the Porter in *Macbeth*; and the wail of more modern critics over the "parochial" dinginess of Ibsen's world. But for true genius few things are irredeemably common or unclean. It is the treatment that matters.

Tragedy, once more, represents "an action which is complete in itself": but then what constitutes completeness? Here lies already the apple of discord between Classic and Romantic, between the completeness of *Antony and Cleopatra* and the differing completeness of *Bérénice*. And then, again, there is that more modern view which rejects the ideal of completeness altogether in favour of *une tranche de vie*.

"Expressed in speech made beautiful"—this too is changed to-day, when our playwrights wrestle above the grave of verse drama with the question whether even the prose of their predecessors is not too stylized and beautiful to represent a world where people speak without any style at all.

"Acted, not narrated"—but this is only partly true even of Greek tragedy. Not everything permits itself to be acted. "Let not Medea slay her sons before the audience"; things like that, at least, on the Greek stage were relegated to a Messenger's Speech. They were too horrible to show. Here again a gulf opens between Sophocles and Shakespeare, between Webster and Racine—precisely how much shall be enacted, how much related? What is too horrible? The Unities, too, lurk here in ambush—are we to perform, or to narrate, what happened three days ago, ten miles away?[1]

And so, last of all, we come to the famous statement of the final end of Tragedy—that Purgation or "*Catharsis*" of the emotions, so glibly bandied about by critics and journalists, so endlessly misunderstood, so uncritically assumed to be true.

Enough has been said to show what a cockpit of criticism this memorable definition of tragedy has been, ever since the *Poetics* came back to the world at the Renaissance—to bring certainty and salvation at last, so men fondly dreamed, to an art long lost in medieval darkness.

To-day if we tried to remould the definition of Aristotle it might run, perhaps, simply thus: "Serious drama is a serious representation by speech and action of some phase of human life." If there is an unhappy ending, we may call it a tragedy; but if the play is a serious attempt to represent life, it makes no great difference whether or not good fortune intervenes in the last scene. Can we say more? This bare tautology is all that really remains of Aristotle's famous formula. The rest of his stipulations, though all of them have still some force, have all been broken at some time or other. The serious-

[1] True, tragic Messengers are also actors, and act their narratives; but their narratives are a convention to avoid acting things too remote, difficult, or horrifying. They become more like the reciters of epic.

ness of Tragedy has become mingled with comic relief; the ideals of completeness, of beauty in language and metre, of the purgation of pity and fear—all these have been successfully challenged. But though Aristotle's laws have been broken, their history is the history of Tragedy.

III

THE EMOTIONAL EFFECT OF TRAGEDY

The immense controversy, carried on in books, pamph-
lets, sheets, and flying articles, mostly German, as to what
it was that Aristotle really meant by the famous words in
the sixth chapter of the *Poetics*, about tragedy accomplish-
ing the purification of our moods of pity and sympathetic
fear, is one of the disgraces of the human intelligence, a
grotesque monument of sterility.

JOHN MORLEY, Diderot

WHAT is indeed the function of Tragedy? This, for
instance, is what it could offer to an Elizabethan
audience.

> The rawish dank of clumsy winter ramps
> The fluent summer's vein; and drizzling sleet
> Chilleth the wan bleak cheek of the numb'd earth,
> Whilst snarling gusts nibble the juiceless leaves
> From the nak'd, shudd'ring branch; and pills the skin
> From off the soft and delicate aspects.
> O now, methinks, a sullen, tragic scene
> Would suit the time with pleasing congruence. . . .
>   Therefore, we proclaim,
> If any spirit breathes within this round,
> Uncapable of weighty passion
> (As from his birth being hugg'd in the arms,
> And nuzzled 'twixt the breasts of happiness),
> Who winks, and shuts his apprehension up

From common sense of what men were and are,
Who would not know what men must be—let such
Hurry amain from our black-visaged shows:
We shall affright their eyes. But if a breast
Nail'd to the earth with grief; if any heart
Pierc'd through with anguish pant within this ring;
If there be any blood whose heat is choked
And stifled with true sense of misery;
If ought of these strains fill this consort up—
Th' arrive most welcome.

(MARSTON, Prologue to *Antonio's Revenge*)

Here is a curious way, surely, of enjoying an afternoon. Confronted with such a performance an impartial stranger from another planet might well exclaim: "You groan perpetually about the ills and woes of your life on earth. You have reason. But why, in the moments when you are not actually suffering, do you choose to go and suffer in imagination?" And that devotee of the *Poetics*, A. B. Walkley, with admirable suavity would have answered for humanity in the classic words of the definition we have quoted: "As Aristotle has said, in order that by pity and fear we may effect the *Catharsis* or purgation of such emotions."

So Aristotle has said, and that has long sufficed. Indeed the *Catharsis* does yeoman service still: if we dislike A's poem or B's play, we need only say impressively that they fail to produce "the right cathartic effect". It is much simpler than giving reasons. So it was that the professor silenced the fishwife by calling her an isosceles triangle.

Here emerge three problems of much psychological interest: first—"what was really Aristotle's view?"; secondly—"how far is it true?"; thirdly—"what led him to adopt it?"

First, there has been age-long controversy about Aristotle's meaning, though it has almost always been accepted that whatever he meant was profoundly right. Many, for example, have translated *catharsis* as "purification", "correction or refinement", "Reinigung", "Veredlung", or the like. It has been suggested that our pity and fear are "purified" in the theatre by becoming disinterested. It is bad to be selfishly sentimental, timid, and querulous; but it is good to pity Othello or to fear for Hamlet. Our selfish emotion has been "sublimated". All this is most edifying; but it does not appear to be what Aristotle intended.

There is strong evidence that *catharsis* means, not "purification", but "purgation". A medical metaphor. (Aristotle was the son of a physician.) Yet, owing to changes in medical thought, "purgation" has become radically misleading to modern minds. Inevitably we think of purgatives, and *complete* evacuations of waste products; and then outraged critics ask why our emotions should be so ill-treated.

But *catharsis* means "purgation", not in the modern, but in the older, wider English sense which included the *partial* removal of excess "humours". The theory is as old as the School of Hippocrates that on a due balance (συμμετρία) of these humours

37

depended the health of body and mind alike.[1] As with Shakespeare's Brutus—

> His life was gentle, and the *Elements*
> So mixt in him, that Nature might stand up,
> And say to all the world; This was a man.

It is "purgation" in Aristotle's sense when Lyly speaks of "the roote Rubarbe, which beeinge full of choler, purgeth choler"; when Webster's Duke Ferdinand cries "Rubarbe, oh, for rubarbe To purge this choller!"; or when Shakespeare's Richard II exclaims "Let's purge this choller without letting blood." For "purgation" included blood-letting; where no one would have dreamed of removing *all* the blood. Similarly, in Greek, Aristotle uses the corresponding verb, *apocathairesthai*, of the relief of sexual tension by coition; and his disciple Theophrastus applies *catharsis* even to the pruning of trees —with the same idea of moderating excess.

In fine, "the *catharsis* of such passions" does *not* mean that the passions are purified and ennobled,

---

[1] Pity, in particular, was associated with excess of wetness (cf. tears); and fear with excess of cold (it chills). Old gentlemen, Aristotle thought, are timider, because chillier. (See H. Flashar, *Die medizinischen Grundlagen der Lehre von der Wirkung der Dichtung in der griechischen Poetik*, in *Hermes*, 84 (1956), 12-48.) Gorgias (c. 483-376) had already compared words to drugs that can remove the body's humours. If mental states were thus linked with bodily states, it was natural enough to conclude that mental states were likewise open to medical treatment—often of a homeopathic kind. Cf. Plato, *Timaeus*, 86-9; *Laws*, 790 (Bacchants calmed by dance and music, as infants by rocking and crooning); *Sophist*, 230 (the self-opinionated purged by cross-questioning); *Phaedo*, 66-7.

nice as that might be; it does *not* mean that men are purged of their passions; it means simply that the passions themselves are reduced to a healthy, balanced proportion.[1]

A passage in Aristotle's *Politics* (viii. 7. 5-6) makes clearer his general idea. There, speaking of the value of music, he says: "Passions which affect some temperaments violently, occur to some extent in all. There is simply a difference of intensity; so, for instance, with pity and fear, and again with religious ecstasy.[2] By this last emotion some minds can be overpowered; yet we see their balance restored by sacred music of an orgiastic type,[3] as if they had received medical treatment (ἰατρεία) and *catharsis*.[4]

---

[1] "Purgation", with the disappearance of the "humours" and of blood-letting, has become an unhappily misleading translation. "Moderating" or "tempering" of the passions keeps the sense, but loses the metaphor. Perhaps "healthy relief" might serve. W. Hamilton Fyfe (*Aristotle's Art of Poetry*, XVI) quotes a letter of Byron's: "Poetry is the lava of the imagination, whose eruption prevents an earthquake."

[2] ἐνθουσιασμός (lit. "being possessed by a god"). The corresponding verb is used by Plato (*Ion*, 535c) of the passionate pity and fear felt by the Homeric reciter.

[3] Banned by Plato (*Republic*, 398-9).

[4] This may seem a little fantastic. But cf. Michelet, *Histoire de France* (1879 ed.), VI. 116-7: "The Portuguese chronicle tells us that the king, Don Pedro, in his terrible grief for Ines de Castro which lasted till his death, felt a strange need of dancing and music. There were only two things left that he loved—tortures and concerts. These last had, for him, to be violent and stunning, played by metallic instruments whose piercing tone must become tyrannically dominant, drowning the inner voices of the soul and making the body move like an automaton. Specially for this end he employed long trumpets of silver. Sometimes, when sleepless, he

Similarly with those prone to pity, or to fear, or to emotion generally—in so far as they are subject to such passionate states, they can all undergo a kind of *catharsis* and find in it a pleasurable alleviation." One may compare David playing to Saul. Emotion is relieved by emotional art.[1]

According to Aristoxenus (born, at Tarentum, from ten to twenty-five years after Aristotle) this use of music went back to the Pythagoreans; who, he says (rightly or wrongly), "practised the *catharsis* of the body by medicine, of the soul by music".

"But," the intelligent reader may ask, "granted that emotions like pity and fear in real life are to be healthily moderated by pity and fear in the theatre, what exactly does Aristotle mean by *that*? Fear of what? Pity for what? Have men too much pity? *Could* they have too much?" As the shrewd and lively Fontenelle wrote long ago (*Réflexions sur la Poétique*, xlv): "Je n'ai jamais entendu la purgation des passions par le moyen des passions mêmes; ainsi je n'en dirai rien. Si quelqu'un est purgé par cette voie-là, à la bonne heure; encore ne vois-je pas trop bien à quoi il peut être bon d'être guéri de la pitié."

Aristotle might, I think, have answered that there

would call out his trumpeters by torchlight and go dancing down the streets. Then his people would rise too; and, whether from compassion, or from southern excitability, they would all fall to dancing —king and people together—till he had his fill and dawn brought him home, exhausted, to his palace."

[1] Cf. Milton, Preface to *Samson Agonistes*: "so in physic, things of melancholic hue and quality are used against melancholy, sour against sour, salt to remove salt humours".

are few things, however good, of which one cannot have too much. For example, statesmen, generals, judges, doctors, parents, may all have at times to steel their hearts and become for the moment, however reluctantly, relentless. Some may recall Stefan Zweig's *Beware of Pity*, where a man is softened to undertake more than he can carry through. Further, pity is of more than one kind. There is the useful pity that takes action: there is the useless pity that uses itself up in being felt. Of this there can easily be too much. (Contrast, for instance, Goldsmith and Sterne.) Again, there is pity for oneself. That Aristotle had this too in mind, seems perfectly possible if we remember that he is answering Plato, who had denounced (*Republic*, 603-4) the eloquent lamentations of poets as undermining that fortitude with which in real life the wise and good will bear such sorrows as the loss of a son. Tragedy may, in effect, say to the spectator, as the Circe of Morris to Medea—

Weep not, nor pity thine own life too much.

Then there is fear. Is it (1) fear of horrors on the stage, such as the Erinyes of Aeschylus (supposed to have made women miscarry with terror in the theatre), or the Ghost in Hamlet? Or (2) sympathetic fear for the characters? As when, to take a grotesque example, the rustic spectator shouts to Caesar among the conspirators—"Look out! They are armed." Or (3) a general dread of the ubiquitous cruelty of life, the ruthlessness of human destiny?

I suspect that the first of these—stage-terror—plays a comparatively rare and trivial part.

> Terrify babes, my Lord, with painted devils,
> I am past such needlesse palsy.

Fear of the second kind—sympathetic fear for the characters—is specifically mentioned by Aristotle (xiii. 2). And by allowing free vent to this in the theatre, I take it men are to lessen, in facing life thereafter, their own fear of the third kind—their general dread of destiny. For I hesitate to suppose that Aristotle could possibly have expected them to be made more courageous, say, about rescuing drowning infants from rivers.

> The thoughts of others
> Were light and fleeting,
> Of lovers' meeting
> Or luck or fame.
> Mine were of trouble,
> And mine were steady,
> So I was ready
> When trouble came.
>
> (A. E. HOUSMAN)

"People," I once heard it said, "who dislike *Troilus and Cressida* are afraid of life." I suspect it is sometimes true.

Modern men are apt to groan about the menaces overhanging civilization. But many a Greek was, perforce, still more conscious of living dangerously. For the Athenian standing on his own Acropolis, to westward across the Saronic Gulf loomed the citadel of often hostile Corinth, to northward frowned Parnes, the mountain-frontier of often hostile Boeotia. His city lay in full view of her enemies. His medical science was primitive. His expectation of life remained far less than ours. We are sometimes too sorry for ourselves. Again, the Greeks, though often bursting with vitality, were seldom optimists. Their literature was not lacking in suggestions that it is better not to be born; that the best gift of the gods to those they love is death in youth; that man is the unhappiest creature upon the face of earth. It seems not unreasonable for Aristotle to picture the tragic spectator who had trembled for Œdipus or Cassandra, as leaving the theatre in a mood—

> From too much love of living,
> From hope and fear set free.

Too often, however, it is misleadingly assumed that the *only* emotions supposed by Aristotle to find healthy relief in serious drama are pity and fear. But he does not say "by pity and fear producing the relief of *these* emotions"[1]; he says "the relief of *such* emotions"—"of emotions of *that sort*". But of what sort? I take it that a tragic audience has also such feelings as sympathy and repugnance, delight and indignation, admiration and contempt. To Aristotle, presumably, these seemed less important, or less intense. But how are *they* relieved "by means of pity and fear"? I can only suppose something like this.

---

[1] Though some scholars have maintained (wrongly, I think) that such is in fact the meaning.

Imagine a person whose emotional energy becomes dammed up like water in a reservoir. At a play his sympathetic anxiety and pity act as the two *main* pipes that safely lower his *general* level of emotionalism. Or think of his general emotional tension as an electric charge which finds its discharge by these two main conductors. Odd; but it seems to me, psychologically, not unsound.

Compare the closing lines of *Samson Agonistes*—

> His servants He, with new acquist
> Of true experience from this great event,
> With peace and consolation hath dismissed,
> And calm of mind, *all* passion spent.

So too with the verdict of Manoah—

> Nothing is here for tears, nothing to wail
> Or knock the breast; no weakness, no contempt,
> Dispraise, or blame; nothing but well and fair,
> And what may quiet us in a death so noble.

Grief, weakness, contempt, blame—these I take to be the sort of thing that Aristotle meant by "feelings of that sort."

Much modern criticism is maddening when read critically, because it persistently reads into dead writers subtleties, complications, and implications which anyone historically-minded must regard with the most suspicious scepticism. I am anxious not to do that with Aristotle. But with the *Poetics*, a collection of memoranda both abbreviated and incomplete —the detailed explanation of *catharsis* promised elsewhere (*Politics*, viii. 7. 4) seems to have come in the part now missing—we are forced back on conjecture. And if Aristotle did not mean something like this, I do not know what he meant.

It seems likely, though Aristotle's theory of Comedy is lost, that it was the twin of this; and that as Tragedy in Aristotle's view rids us of excess in emotions like pity and fear, Comedy performs the same service for emotions less polite, both the aggressiveness, the love of ridicule, the *Schadenfreude*, which make us desire to abuse and deride our neighbours, and also the appetites of sex, "the good gross earth" at the roots of human nature. The comic festivals of Athens with their phallic element gave an outlet, like the Roman Saturnalia and the medieval Feast of Fools, to all the Rabelais in man. And after witnessing in the work of Aristophanes and his fellow-dramatists a wild whirl of bawdry and scurrility, after seeing Cleon basted or Lysistrata triumphant, cobbler and lamp-maker went home to live as decent and law-abiding citizens of Athens till the next carnival of this kind came round.

One should not, of course mistake Aristotle's definition of tragedy to mean that he thought *catharsis* the one and only function of drama. Detached passages in the *Poetics* seem sometimes no more exhaustive than the detached jottings of Samuel Butler's admirable *Notebooks*. In this treatise Aristotle has an unmethodical way of scattering his views on some dramatic point in half a dozen different places. And so elsewhere, in moments less austere, he men-

tions also what to most of us seems more important
in drama—its pleasures; the pleasure of *catharsis*
itself, of emotion relieved; the pleasure of artistic
representation; the pleasures of style, metre, and
music; the pleasure also (though it should remain
subordinate) of scenic effects.

Nor need the moral effects of drama be taken as
confined to *catharsis*. Of music Aristotle says
(*Politics*, viii. 4-7) that some serves for education,
some for *catharsis*, some for recreation. "Rhythms
and melodies," he adds, "can very exactly represent
anger and gentleness; courage, self-control, and their
opposites; and all other moral qualities. . . . Clearly,
therefore, music has a definite influence on
character." Even painting, he thinks, has like,
though lesser, effects—the young should look at
works by the idealizing Polygnotus, not by the de-
basing Pauson. Presumably, then, he thought
tragedy too must influence men directly by the fineness of characters like Prometheus or Antigone, as
well as by the healthful relief of *catharsis*.

Still the stress on this remains; and some will be
irritated that a critic should make all this pother
about mental health. There I cannot agree. Much of
our criticism, obsessed with pleasure-values and
blind to influence-values, seems to me frivolously
irresponsible (with eccentric exceptions like Tolstoy)
towards the vital effect of books in making their
readers saner or sillier, more balanced or more un-
balanced, more civilized or more barbarian. That
Plato and Aristotle gave so much thought to the

relation between works of art and mental health, appears to me admirable; whether or no one agrees with all their conclusions.[1]

Such, then, is the famous theory of *Catharsis*, so long and widely accepted, so often quoted, less often understood. It is certainly very odd. Let us lay aside for the moment both our familiarity with the idea and our reverence for the writer, and think. Suppose one asked some queue-waiter: "Why are you standing two and a half hours in the rain to see this thing? Is it that you need your emotions purged?" In the words of Hamlet, "For you to put him to his purgation would perhaps plunge him into far more choler." Or suppose we said: "I have not wept properly for three months, so to-night I shall relieve my pent-up feelings by going to the most lachrymose drama I can find"; should we expect to be taken seriously? Of course the function of Tragedy might quite well be what Aristotle says, without the average spectator being aware of it. Aristotle is speaking as moralist and legislator. The popular attraction of Tragedy may be that appropriate pleasure, which, as Aristotle him-

[1] For others, Aristotle's *catharsis* is not ethical enough—too concerned with mental health rather than morals. Hence the attempts to render it "purification" or "sublimation"; and a recent suggestion (House, *Poetics*, 104-111) that it directs our pity and fear *"towards worthy objects"*. But in discussing music (*Pol.* viii. 7) Aristotle clearly *contrasts* the kind that is educational with the kind that is *cathartic* (such as the emotional flute). For him, I think, serious drama may in general improve the *quality* and direction of our pity or fear; but its strictly *cathartic* effect simply tempers their *quantity* to healthy balance. One may not like Aristotle's view: but one should not twist it.

self says, it is also its business to give; yet the actual benefit of Tragedy might none the less be this purgation from excess of emotions like pity and fear.

Yet is it? That is our second question. The theory strikes me as very strange. Do we really, for example, suffer from pent-up surpluses of compassion?

"But surely," an ardent Aristotelian might answer, "such emotional accumulations do occur. The Chinese, said Keyserling, though usually self-controlled, were prone to storms of bull-fury about nothing, which they ascribed to accumulation of 'Ch'i', the substance of anger; just as Ibsen's pet scorpion grew ill unless it could periodically vent its venom on a piece of fruit. Similarly tears, like blood-letting, relieve the blood-pressure on an over-wrought brain. For a visible embodiment of *catharsis*, look at Botticelli's 'Mars and Venus'—the fierce War-god, after his blaze of lover's passion, lies at peace, while little Loves play with his weapons of death."[1]

Answer. Certainly men may suffer from accumulated tensions of some forms of impulse—tensions of aggressiveness, of physical desire, of energy and emotionalism in general. There is a good deal to be said for Aristotle's *catharsis* as a partial justification of Aristophanes or the Saturnalia, broad comedy or carnival. One might even make a case for regarding the Romantic Revival as a vast *catharsis* after the cramping inhibitions of the "Age of Reason"— though it might be questioned if its effects were very

[1] Cf. *Problemata*, IV. 30.

healthful. But about tragedy I remain dubious. Here few emotions, if any, are so dominant as pity. Yet I cannot trace in myself beforehand any excessive urge to pity, that presses for relief; and I should have thought the effect of reading, say, Hardy's tragic novels was to make men, not less compassionate, but more. Consider that amusing passage of Marivaux on the Parisian character: "It is soul-stirring emotions that this populace demands—the stronger, the better. They long to pity you, if you are outraged; to feel compassion for you, if you are injured; to tremble for your life, if you are menaced. That is their delight. And if your enemy had not space enough to beat you, they would make room of their own accord, without meaning any harm, and would gladly call to him—'Go on, beat him at your ease, don't deprive us of any of the pleasure we feel in shuddering for the poor wretch'. . . . *That* stirs their souls, which never know anything, have never seen anything before, are always quite new to everything."

One *could*, of course, argue that these good folk were instinctively craving a *catharsis*. But I should have thought they were suffering in their daily lives, not from excess of emotion, but from deficiency; that they wanted, not to be "purged", but to be fed—that they were hungry and thirsty for emotions that the dull round of their days denied.

No doubt one could define dining as a purgation of excessive hunger and thirst. But that would be rather topsy-turvy. Surely there is a real difference

49

between a body too full-blooded, that needs to be relieved, and a starving one that needs to be replenished? Between suffering from too much thyroid, and from too little?

In modern civilization many are condemned to live like the married couple in Prior—

> Without Love, Hatred, Joy or Fear,
> They led—a kind of—as it were:
> Nor Wish'd nor Car'd nor Laugh'd nor Cry'd:
> And so they liv'd: and so they dy'd.

For the ordinary citizen the danger is not that his emotions will burst him like the dragon of Babylon, but that they will atrophy into apathy as with the woman who said to the district-visitor: "The truth is me and my husband aren't interested in anything." Young French Romantics may have gone about with their hands pressed to their hearts, lest they explode: but I suspect that genuine Emily Brontës have always been rare.

Aristotle's theory may have been truer for an excitable Mediterranean race. But I remain doubtful In his *Ethics* (II. 6. 10-11) Aristotle himself says (as one would expect from the Philosopher of Moderation): "Fear and boldness, desire, anger, and pity, and pleasure or pain in general, can be felt both more and less than they should be." That is, he recognises that we may have too little feeling as well as too much. But in the *catharsis* of the *Poetics* he seems to ignore this. For *catharsis* cannot, so far as I know, be used of remedying defect—only of reducing excess.

It would have been truer, I think, if he had defined serious drama as "providing by means of pity, sympathy, and other emotions a relief, exercise, and sustenance for the emotional side of human nature". And even that would be only part of the truth.

"Yet consider," our Aristotelian might retort, "how strikingly Aristotle has been justified by modern psychology in seeing the danger of emotional repressions, the need for emotional outlets.

"Here, for example, is a man who has lost the woman he loved to another. But he is resolved to keep a stoic impassiveness, to say calmly 'Good riddance!', to put her wholly from his mind. But he is lying to himself. Man cannot always escape his share of sorrow. The mental wound he would not face transforms itself neurotically into physical illness. Plato's bluntly repressive attitude towards human emotions can prove dangerously unwise.

"On the other hand, when Egil Skallagrimsson resolved to starve to death after losing his sons at sea, his daughter Thorgerd saved the old man by beguiling him first to compose a lament for the dead. Art relieved the intolerable grief. Writers like Goethe or Poe found a similar remedy by putting into fiction what reality had denied them. Plays like Cocteau's *Enfants Terribles* or Hauptmann's *Vor Sonnenuntergang* have helped others to live out tormenting impulses in fantasy, or to allay the guilt of feeling themselves uniqely depraved. In group-therapy patients have been enabled to release emotions repressed from consciousness by acting them out dramatically.

Indeed Freud himself in early days used the term
Catharsis, until he found that release of emotion was
not enough, unless the repressions were also
analysed."[1]

Answer. These analogies are fascinating, but un-
historical. Doubtless Aristotle was saner in this than
Plato with his phobia of emotion. But he could know
nothing of the Unconscious or of "repression" in
the Freudian sense.

Besides, the remedy is not so simple. The appetite
for emotion may grow with the eating. Augustine's
friend Alypius had a horror of gladiatorial shows;
dragged to one, he hid his eyes; yet he ended with a
blood-lust for them. It can happen with bull-fighting
(so that Gautier pronounced its moments of supreme
tension "worth all the drama of Shakespeare"). And
notice how the trailers of films make their appeal by
promises of ever more stupendous passion, more
blood-curdling horror, or more sexual audacity.
Plato might have smiled—and shuddered.

Again, those who enjoy such fantasies may wish to
act them out in reality; or, on the contrary, seeking
emotions in unreality may end by having only unreal
emotions—like Louis XIV, melted by Racine's *Esther*,
yet ruthlessly ordering the devastation of the Rhine-
land, the hounding of Huguenots in the Cevennes.

True, Aristotle had in mind drama of a high order,
acted only at dramatic festivals on a few days each
year; he might have regarded us, with our plays and
films all the year round, as dramatic dipsomaniacs.

[1] See my *Literature and Psychology*, 274-9.

But then one may wonder if dramatic emotions limited to a few days could really much affect men's characters for the rest of the twelve months.[1] Further, if tragedy can have a calmative effect, may not this be largely due to causes more intellectual? May it not be that it can remould our whole view of life towards something larger, braver, less self-centred— towards "the sad science of renunciation"? Montaigne's Mexicans used to greet the new-born with the words—"Child, you have come into the world to endure; endure, suffer, and be silent."[2] In great drama we hear that warning repeated with the wisdom and eloquence of master-minds.

To conclude, the theory of *catharsis* seems to me interesting, and not without some truth; but far less profound than critical mystery-mongering has tried to make it. If one were pleading before the government of some new Utopia, against some new Rousseau, in favour of allowing drama, it would be unwise, I think, to base one's case very much on the doctrine of *catharsis*.

What, then, led Aristotle to adopt it? Really to understand his attitude we must, I think, understand two other things—the Greek view of life, and Plato's.

Ever since man began to reason as well as to

---

[1] It has, however, to be remembered that Greek plays were also a good deal read. (For example, in Aristophanes, *Frogs*, 52-3, Dionysus speaks of reading Euripides' *Andromeda* even at sea on naval service.)

[2] Cf. W. Stekel, *Impulshandlungen*, 504: "The enemy of humanity is Utopia. The most vital task of the educator is to educate towards reality."

desire, he has been eternally tormented by the conflict within him between the spirit and the flesh.
What is to be done with the passions? "Subdue them
by abstinence" has been the answer of the ascetic, of
Plato and the Stoics, of Buddha and of Christ.
"Govern them by reasonable indulgence" was the
instinctive reply of the Greek and the reasoned conclusion of Aristotle. It may be better to enter heaven
maimed than not at all; but how loathsome to be
maimed! "Into Paradise go these same old priests,
and halt old men and maimed, who all day and night
cower continually before the altars, and in the crypts;
and such folk as wear old amices and old clouted
frocks, and naked folk and shoeless, and covered
with sores, perishing of hunger and thirst, and of
cold, and of little ease. These be they that go into
Paradise, with them have I naught to make." In that
cry of Aucassin against medieval asceticism the
Hellene lives again. Through the clear air of that
smaller, less complicated Greek world we see this
problem, like so many others, sharply set and
answered. There, face to face, stand arrayed the
opposite ideals—Apollo and Dionysus, the god of
Dorian discipline and the god of the licence of the
wild. Yet both are Greek, both lay claim to wisdom:
and instead of burning the votaries of Dionysus at
the stake, when he came storming on a wave of
enthusiasm from the fastnesses of Thrace, the priests
of Apollo gave his untamed younger brother, the son
likewise of Zeus, a share in Apollo's temple beneath
the twin crags of Delphi. That reconciliation is

typical of Greek balance, clarity, and good sense—
"nothing too much", not even righteousness. They
had learned the priceless secret of casting out devils
by Beelzebub; and when the nurse urges Phædra in
Hippolytus that over-scrupulousness is not good for
man, that the beam which bears the heavy roof must
needs sag below perfect straightness, she is, though
a devil, quoting Greek scripture. And if Phædra's
looseness there brings disaster, so also does the over-
strictness of Hippolytus himself. Such, in brief, is
the Hellenic view of life, which has so long done
battle with the opposite creed of the Hebrew in
Western civilization.

Into this Greek world, however, was born a great
man, who only half belonged to it, Plato. In him
appear that hunger and thirst for righteousness, that
sense of sin, that need for dogma—a sort of philosophic sacerdotalism—which seem to us not typically
Greek, because in Greece, though present, they
failed to win the upper hand. As Plato grew older,
these things grew stronger in him, until he became
the transcendent paradox we know, a supreme artist
denouncing art as wicked. Art, he cried, is bad
because it is but the imitation of an imitation of the
eternally existent reality; poetry is bad because it tells
lies, and fails to teach men that the world is a place
of perfect justice; and it is again bad because it encourages the emotions. It is, first, unreal; secondly,
unrighteous; thirdly, unrestrained. And so poets are
banished without mercy from his ideal Republic.
Plato, like Pentheus, did not love Dionysus. "The

natural hunger for weeping and lamentation, which we keep under control in our own hours of unhappiness, is just what your poets gratify and indulge." "Poetry feeds and waters the passions, weeds that should rather be killed by drought."[1] And, among the different kinds of poetry, drama is particularly bad because the actors, in representing a variety of other characters, destroy their own. The long Puritan attack on the stage has begun—part of that larger effort of those who see all things as either right or wrong, either white or black, to wash out the colour from the world.

Now it is this attitude of his master's that Aristotle is here concerned to answer, though without ever mentioning that master's name. The poet, Plato had argued in his *Ion*, creates in an inspired ecstasy, bereft of his sober senses. (And poets and critics have naïvely taken this as a compliment ever since.) Vain therefore to trust the fuddled judgments of this divine drunkard: trust only the philosopher. Art, Plato had continued in his *Republic*, is the idle shadow of a shadow, twice removed from true reality.[2] Poetry, retorts Aristotle (ix. 3), is something *more* philosophic and serious than history.[3] Poetry,

[1] *Republic*, 606 A and D.

[2] This nicety always seems to me a little comic in a thinker who himself included among instruments of government the noble lie; and very curious in a writer who himself composed some of the most charming of myths.

[3] For example, the Cleon of Aristophanes has eclipsed the Cleon of history; he has become an eternal *type* of the Demagogue. Shakespeare's Antony has become far more real for most men than the historic Marcus Antonius; Polonius than Lord Burleigh.

said Plato, makes men cowardly by its pictures of the afterworld. No, replies Aristotle, it can purge men's fears. Poetry, said Plato, encourages men to be hysterical and uncontrolled. On the contrary, answers his pupil, it makes them less, not more, emotional, by giving a periodic and healthy outlet to their feelings. In short, Aristotle's definition of tragedy is half a defence. This reply is, indeed, part of Aristotle's general reaction from Plato—"kicking out like a colt at its mother", as Plato is said to have complained. Aristotle's insistence on what seems to us an insignificant feature of tragedy seems, in brief, to be explained as an ingenious piece of special pleading—an argument *ad hominem*. He stands in the position of a person arguing with a fanatical Puritan about wine or dancing. The advocate of moderate indulgence is naturally driven to plead that wine is good medicinally and dancing as exercise; but, in fact, men do not usually drink wine as medicine, and only a Socrates dances alone in his house for exercise.

But the question remains—why do men trouble to write and act and watch plays that, even if they do not end in unhappiness, are full of agony and disaster? Why do we try to make seem as real as possible things that, if real, would be unbearable? Aristotle has answered Plato: but he has not really answered this. If we asked the dramatists in Elysium —unless Tragedy is there a clean forgotten thing— their replies, we may be sure, would widely disagree. What was Tragedy to Æschylus? A means of uttering his exultation in human greatness and heroism, his troubled groping to find the gods behind the gods, the hidden springs of the justice of the world. To Sophocles? Sophocles might answer us, as in the old story he answered the court that tried him on his son's charge of senility, by reading one of his choruses—not, as then, the chorus of *Œdipus at Colonus* in praise of Athens, but that other chorus from *Antigone*, of which the theme is the marvellousness of man. For him, we feel, that was the supreme thing: though not for Euripides, driven by that gnawing hunger for truth which troubles beauty, furrowing with thought the lines upon her face; angered to sting his hearers as well as to please them; struggling always not to purge them of over-pity, but to teach them more. And Shakespeare? His feeling we may fancy much the same as that of Sophocles. *Hamlet* might answer *Antigone* with its echo of the same cry—"What a piece of work is a man!" With Racine,[1] a different and self-conscious theory finds expression in the preface to *Phèdre*: there he speaks as though he loved the Tragic Muse less as a mistress than as a school-mistress; and yet we should never have guessed it from his work. *Phèdre* as a drunken helot! We feel only the pity of it; and the failure of the moralist is the triumph of the tragedian. Then if we turn last to a dramatist who seems far more

[1] Cf. Grimm, writing of Letourneur's *Shakespeare* (1776-82) and contrasting the English theatre with the French: "The whole effort of the one seems directed to excite the liveliest passions; the whole effort of the other to calm them and restore them to their natural course."

purposeful and propagandist than Racine and more like Euripides, we shall find Ibsen on the contrary affirming that his aim is, above all, to be an artist. We might search farther but we should only find the same disagreement, in theory, among those who have written tragedy; and in practice, among them all the same passionate interest—their one common feeling—not in purgations, but in human beings.

Pass from the poets to the philosophers and the critics. They will answer us with none of the uncertainty or the brevity of the poets; they know the end and function of tragedy without the shadow of a doubt. Unfortunately they all disagree. To begin with, a mass of criticism from ancient almost to modern times has taken the simple view that poetry gives moral lessons. In the eyes of Aristophanes, Hesiod taught men husbandry, Homer war, Æschylus courage to die for one's country; even to Johnson, Shakespeare remained, like Euripides, a treasury of political and moral philosophy.[1] But to-day, when Homer's tactics are out of date and Shakespeare is attacked for his want of original ideas, we have grown to expect, not to be instructed by poetry, but to enjoy it. Pleasure has come to be the admitted end of art; men write tragedy and read it because they like it; and there—for most—is an end of the matter. But there remains the psychological problem

---

[1] John Dennis is particularly explicit: "Every tragedy ought to be a very solemn lecture, inculcating a particular providence, and showing it plainly protecting the good and chastising the bad."

—why do they like it? And over this the theorists quarrel even more.

Rousseau, looking back, beyond Aristotle, to Plato and forward to Tolstoy, renews in mid eighteenth century, from his own Arcadian standpoint, the attacks of early medieval and Renaissance Churches against the stage. In 1757 d'Alembert (with Voltaire behind him) had urged Geneva to permit the theatre[1]: in 1759 the Genevan Rousseau retorted with his *Lettre sur les Spectacles*.

For him, civilization was corrupt; arts and sciences had brought evil; and particularly evil was the theatre. Actors are immoral, actresses worse;[2] tragedy is depraving, comedy worse. He had no use for Diderot's view (like Shaw's) of stage as pulpit. In Rousseau's eyes tragedy is a mere pastime, which provokes at best a fugitive and futile pity "without ever producing the least humane act"; "it makes us applaud our own courage in the process of praising the courage of others". Even if it fills us with passion against evil characters, it still fills us with passion; whereas the only true purge for passions is reason, which finds no place on the stage. Above all, it encourages amorousness and woman-worship. Titus may give up Bérénice; but the sympathies of the whole audience have wedded her.

Besides, drama is forced to flatter, not correct,

[1] *Encyclopédie*, vol. vii.

[2] Not till 1849, apparently, did the Council of Soissons relieve players of excommunication—70 years after Garrick's burial in Westminster Abbey! Whether orthodoxy showed itself in this ethically superior to its victims, may be doubted.

men's passions and prejudices—or it fails. "It purges the passions one has not, and foments those one has." Thus the dramatist's road to success is, at London, to attack the French; at Tunis, to glorify pirates; at Goa, to celebrate burnings of Jews. Instead of poetic justice, tragedy holds up before us monsters like Catilina, Atrée, Mahomet, Horace stabbing his sister, Syphax poisoning his wife. Médée or Phèdre may be wicked: but we find them less wicked in the fifth act than in the first. Men are amused with such subjects as a son killing his father and marrying his mother, or a father drinking his children's blood. "Gladiatorial massacres were not so barbarous."[1]

In fine, drama is only justified in a corrupt society, which it distracts from employing itself still worse. (Thus Rousseau could excuse his having written for the stage himself.)

There remains a tragic irony in the thought that perhaps none of the drama he denounced was in the end to do as much harm to the world as his own writings; which by their eloquence and passion, rather than by originality of ideas, contributed so potently to Romantic egotism in the individual, and in politics to revolution and state-tyranny. Yet, irritating as Rousseau is, it would be cant, I think, to deny that stage and film *have* often done more for men's pleasure than for their real happiness; or that

[1] Similar arguments follow against comedy (Rousseau had little humour). It flatters the frivolous shrewdness of the worldly in preference to real goodness; as in Molière's *Misanthrope*, which Rousseau attacks at great length (largely, one suspects, because he saw much of himself in its hero).

even good drama can often be bad for fools. Still, when one thinks of *The Oresteia*, or *Hamlet*, or *The Master Builder*, his carpings do not seem very intelligent. Rousseau could charm; he could storm; but often he lacked discrimination.

Next we may turn to the saner Hume.[1] In part he accepts the explanation of the Abbé Dubos, that we go to tragedies because it is pleasanter to be grieved than bored; in part also that of Fontenelle,[2] who argued that the difference between a painful and a pleasant emotion is often merely one of degree. Thus a gentle movement will tickle pleasantly where the same movement more violently performed would hurt. At a play we know that it is only a play, and that knowledge sufficiently weakens our emotions to make what would in real life have been painful, become pleasant. Hume recognized a measure of truth in both these views; but he finds them, as well he might, inadequate. There is too, he urges, the pleasure we feel in the activity of the imagination as it mirrors life. And we feel that pleasure all the more intensely when it is one of the intenser sides of life that is so mirrored. Thus the devastation of Sicily by Verres, to take Hume's own example, was not a fiction, but had actually occurred, and yet the very extent of the calamity made Cicero's hearers all the more responsive to the eloquence of the Verrine Orations which denounced the tyrant. The terrible becomes pleasant in the theatre, said Fontenelle,

[1] *Essays*: "Of Tragedy" (1742).
[2] *Réflexions sur la Poétique*, xxxvi (1742).

simply because its effect is weakened by our sense of its unreality; the imaginative beauty of the play moves us so intensely, replied Hume, just because the subject is terrible. We might put it thus: to Fontenelle the pleasure of watching a tragedy is like being tickled with a dagger; for Hume, our emotion at being tickled with a dagger is intensified when we are told that it is the dagger which has killed a king.

Tragic events, he argues, move in us *natural* emotions—pity, anger, loathing, indignation; but at the same time the beauty of the poet's style and imagination rouses, also, *artistic* emotions. Now the force of our natural feelings can be switched to intensify the force of our artistic feelings; as the electric current from one power-station can be switched to reinforce the current from another. But, Hume adds, these natural emotions must remain subordinate to the artistic; otherwise, as in some drama of excessive horrors, we feel, not pleasure, but pain. Thus Clarendon, he suggests, hurries in his history over the death of Charles I because, for Clarendon's generation, its memories were too terrible for any power of art to redeem; whereas later ages, feeling less for poor Charles, find the final tragedy at Whitehall one of the most enthralling episodes of the whole Civil War.

Here too, we may feel, is truth. Antony does indeed first lay bare the wounds of the bleeding Cæsar that his great speech may go home. But perhaps Hume tends to think a little too much of the part played in Tragedy by eloquence, to be too dazzled by the jewelled words on the finger of the Tragic Muse to see quite steadily the Muse herself. For there are times when she abdicates her purple altogether; times when she has worn the rags of Telephus, the plain petticoat of Hedvig Ekdal. There are tragedies in prose, even prosaic prose.

Then there is Hegel,[1] who, happy man, lived in a purely rational and ideal world, a Heaven which was, however, seemingly divided like the House of Beelzebub against itself; whence the apparent tragedies of human life—yet tragedies only apparent. For all such discords, we are told, merge in a higher harmony at last. Hegel's great example (it squared so well with his theory that he pronounced it the grandest work of ancient or modern times) was *Antigone*. Creon, King of Thebes, had forbidden the burial of Polynices, slain in arms against his country. The dead man's sister Antigone, preferring the laws of God to those of man, buries him notwithstanding and is put to death; but not unavenged, for the same fate overtakes the son and the queen of Creon, leaving him miserable upon a lonely throne. Both king and maiden were right, said Hegel; but they were also both wrong, because not right enough—too onesided in their righteousness. Therefore they both suffer; but the justice of God is done. (Sophocles would have been much surprised to hear it.) That pity which was for Aristotle the very essence of

[1] *Æsthetik* (in *Werke*, Berlin, 1832-40), vol. x. 3 (1838), 527 ff. More accessible is Hegel, *The Philosophy of Fine Art*, transl. F. P. B. Osmaston (1920).

tragedy, is for Hegel merely an insult to the tragic hero or heroine. Their greatness is above our ignorant compassion. They cannot accept more than our general sympathy; for they know that to each his desert is given, and whatever is, is well. Other examples of such a conflict in which righteousness is opposed to righteousness, were found by Hegel in the plays which deal with Agamemnon's sacrifice of his daughter to the cause of Greece at Aulis, or with Orestes' murder of his mother to avenge his sire; and he points out that in the latter instance or, again, in the tale of Philoctetes, the crowning reconciliation occurs, not by the destruction of the individual, but by compromise or submission. He might also have instanced, with more justice than usual, the Prometheus Trilogy with its two great antagonists, Zeus and Prometheus, both guilty of excess at first, in the end both reconciled.

Modern Tragedy, on the other hand, Hegel found less satisfactory; that is to say, less Hegelian. It concentrates too much on the individual character, and its final reconciliations are even less easy to describe as a harmonizing of lower discords in a higher unity.

Such a theory of Tragedy needs no detailed discussion. It is based almost wholly on Greek tragedy. Yet it begins with a travesty of *Antigone*; it goes on to ignore play after play of Æschylus and Sophocles, and it ignores Euripides "the most tragic of the poets". It is easy enough to talk glibly of reconciliation and harmony over the dead bodies on the tragic

stage. It may be true that the cry of the blood of
Agamemnon is satisfied at last with revenge, that
Œdipus comes to rest in a glorious grave in quiet
Colonus, that Heracles ascends to sit on the right
hand of Zeus; but can we suppose that to Cassandra,
to Jocasta, to Dejanira all seemed to end so pleasantly
in a pink sunset of satisfaction? Does the world of
tragedy or the tragedy of the world really bear any
relation to this Universe squirted with philosophic
rose-water? It is an astonishing conception. Many
another Dr Pangloss has endeavoured to make man-
kind swallow the world like a pill by coating it with
sugar; but only Hegel sought his syrup in the heart
of tragedy itself. When the philosopher's Sunday
joint was set smoking before him, we are told that
Hegel used to observe: "Come now, let us fulfil its
destiny"; but few of us will find much comfort as
Phædra, or Deirdre, passes before us to her death, in
"cette doctrine d'oie qu'une oie a pour devoir d'être
un rôti". For Hegel the mere pity for misfortune,
that Virgilian tenderness which cried, "Sunt lacrimæ
rerum et mentem mortalia tangunt", that compassion which to Anatole France seemed to lie at the
very root of the world's great literature—for Hegel
this was the emotion of "country-cousins". How
different is the hero's cry in the lost *Bellerophon* of
Euripides!

Dare any say that there are Gods in Heaven!
There are none, none!—save only for the fool
That still must cling to legends of old time.
Think for yourselves—I do not ask you take

My word on trust. I say men tyrannous,
With tongues that belie all oaths, and hands of robbers,
Fill earth with carnage and with sack of cities;
And, though they do it, prosper more than those
Whose days are spent in peace and piety;
I know of little cities, fearing God,
That yet must bow to wicked greater states,
Crushed by brute weight of spears.[1]

It is strange to reflect, remembering Bacon also, how limited a soul may reside under the mantle of a great philosopher; and yet even Bacon wrote, "The nobler a soul is, the more objects of compassion it hath." In a Utopia peopled by Hegels tragedy might perhaps be what he describes, but that is no concern of ours. His attempt to force his philosophy down the throat of Tragedy as we know it, serves only to provide one more instance of the rashness of metaphysicians who venture into regions where their speculations can for once be checked.

Schopenhauer[2] on the other hand saw Tragedy, like the world it represents, in a very different light. For him the gospel of life is "vanity of vanities"; and tragedies are its parables. When the Chorus of Sophocles cries that it is best never to be born; when the Macaria of Euripides exclaims against the idea of an immortality which would prolong life's agony beyond the peace of death; when Macbeth sees revealed in the white and ghastly light of imminent

[1] Fr. 286; *Greek Drama for Everyman*, 348.
[2] *Die Welt als Wille und Vorstellung* (1819; Eng. trans. by Haldane and Kemp, 7th ed., i. 326-330; iii. 212-219).

death the blank futility of all existence; when Webster cries—

> Pleasure of life, what is't? Only the good houres
> Of an Ague;

at such moments[1] Schopenhauer would recognise with calm satisfaction a reflection and a confirmation of his own vision of the world. And so he came, unreasonably but naturally, to regard such reflections as the great end of Tragedy. We should go home from a play, he thought, having realized more clearly than ever the worthlessness of life, freer than ever from that will to live which Comedy, on the contrary, encourages.

> Ay, look: high heaven and earth ail from the prime
> foundation;
> All thoughts to rive the heart are here, and all are vain:
> Horror and scorn and hate and fear and indignation—
> Oh why did I awake? when shall I sleep again?

This view of Schopenhauer's seems to me far nearer the truth than Hegel's. And it is clear enough that Tragedy (especially in its narrower modern sense—drama with an unhappy ending) is often deeply pessimistic, at least in implication. For we should feel that our emotions had been wrung on false pretences if a choir of angels descended at the close of *Lear* to carry off the old man and his

---

[1] He himself instances the end of Voltaire's *Mahomet* where the dying Palmire cries to the Prophet: "Tu dois régner; le monde est fait pour les tyrans."

daughter into eternal felicity. The Tragic Muse was born of religion, but she has always remained something of an infidel; at least her gods have generally remained as remote and unhelpful as those of Epicurus, except when they have appeared, not to great advantage, in machines. The spectator of drama, says Coleridge, requires a suspension of disbelief; the religious spectator of tragic drama often requires also a suspension of belief.[1] That seldom seems to present much difficulty; but the Church has not readily forgotten or forgiven it. When, however, Schopenhauer implies that tragedies preach, or at all events that tragedies teach, resignation and contempt of life, it is hard to follow him. After all it would be extremely odd if the tragic dramatists of the world all turned out to have been Schopenhauerians in spite of themselves. This feeling of resignation is certainly sometimes the effect of tragedy. "You see that these things must be accomplished thus," says Marcus Aurelius, "and even those endure them who cry out 'O Cithæron!'"[2] But if we had to find a phrase for the mood most generally induced by great tragedy, it would certainly not be resignation or contempt of existence. Life seems at such times infinitely sad, but not worthless; infinitely fragile, yet never more intensely ours. Schopenhauer, indeed, admits that this resigned attitude is not common, even at the end of Greek Tragedy, and explains it by saying that the

[1] For a sincere statement of a much more religious view of tragic drama, see T. R. Henn, *The Harvest of Tragedy*, 1956.
[2] A reference, of course, to *Œdipus Tyrannus*.

Greek dramatists were undeveloped; but this seems suicide for his whole theory. To pretend that the tragedy of Æschylus and Sophocles "has not yet attained to the summit and goal of tragedy" is merely to admit defeat oneself; nor for that matter does modern drama, either, afford many happy examples of his theory.

On Schopenhauer follows Nietzsche's *Birth of Tragedy* (1870-1). For Nietzsche the essence of tragedy is not simple disillusion, but alternate illusion and disillusion. The vision of Apollo builds up before us a heroic world, sublime, magnificent, rejoicing in its splendid individuality.

> A brighter Hellas rears its mountains
>   From waves serener far;
> A new Peneus rolls his fountains
>   Against the morning star.

But with this Apolline vision is combined the wild, self-annihilating rapture of the music of Dionysus. From that tragedy sprang, and in that each tragedy dies away, while the power and the glory and the glamour of this heroic world dissolve in the end ecstatically back to airy nothing. The individual, whom Apollo had bidden above all to know himself here loses himself once more, and rejoices to be lost, in the vast onward Dionysian sweep of life—so ruthless, so exultant, so like a child (said Heraclitus, remembering Homer), building and then overturning its sand-castles on the shore. So a dead leaf might be imagined to rejoice for one final moment when it is torn at last from its twig and whirled away by the year's first south-west gale as it shouts of the coming spring.

E il naufragar m'è dolce in questo mare.

Such seems to be Nietzsche's meaning; but it is hard to be more precise. For to try to understand him is like listening for a coherent answer among the oak groves of Dodona in a hurricane. His book is written in one long intoxication, prefaced by later amendments hardly soberer. When philosophy goes so far, instead of criticizing poetry, it becomes it. But is this, after all, what we go to see in Hamlet—Hamlet who is for Nietzsche the Dionysian man awakened from his visions to see the paralysing futility of life? Yes, sometimes, to some extent. But how complicated, how arbitrary, how constricted such a theory is! Why will the philosophers try to herd the poets, like sheep, all into one narrow pen? Nietzsche's view has indeed this merit, that it sees the effect of tragedy not as a simple thing, but a struggle of opposing feelings— our sense both of the splendour and of the despair of human life.

> We are children of splendour and flame,
>   Of shuddering, also, and tears,
> Magnificent out of the dust we came,
>   And abject from the Spheres.
>   (WILLIAM WATSON).

But if we questioned spectators of tragedy whether they really recognized this pleasurable sense of annihilation, I doubt if many would agree; to which

Nietzsche might reply that it was because their taste was debauched. But that seems no very helpful conclusion.[1]

What, after all, is the upshot of this long debate? Is there no simpler answer? It seems to me a mistake to consider the tragic emotions of drama in such isolation, and apart from the tragic emotions of epic and novel; as if we felt essentially different when we read the death of Hector and of Hamlet, of Desdemona and of Tess of the D'Urbervilles. Surely the main function of all tragic episodes is to satisfy in certain ways our love both of beauty and of truth, of truth to life and about it. Experience, ever more experience is our craving—"Homo sum, nihil humani a me alienum puto." Fortune may starve, and must limit, the adventures we live through as individuals; but we are free at least to dream. "Life piled on life were all too little"; but at least this imaginary

---

[1] Dr I. A. Richards propounded thirty years ago (*Principles of Literary Criticism* (1925), 245 ff.) an ingenious theory that "Pity, the impulse to approach, and Terror, the impulse to retreat, are brought in Tragedy to a reconciliation which they find nowhere else. . . . Their union in an ordered response is the *catharsis* by which Tragedy is recognised, whether Aristotle meant anything of this kind or not." It seems to me inconceivable that Aristotle had any such notion. And I doubt if most theatregoers experience any such fusion of feelings. Further, (1) pity appears to me, in most tragedies, so much more dominant and important than fear that the two could very seldom balance; (2) the fear felt in tragedy is largely sympathetic fear *for* the characters (as Aristotle thought)—but sympathetic fear is scarcely an impulse to *retreat*; (3) Dr Richards dismisses as "pseudo-tragedy" both Greek drama and "almost all Elizabethan tragedy outside Shakespeare's six masterpieces". But a theory so restricted seems hardly a theory of tragedy.

world is there to redress the balance of the real. That is why stories were invented. And since life is often unhappy, so the stories had to be. Even the fairy prince who is to wed the princess and live happily ever after, must suffer first. About the Sleeping Beauty grows the barrier of thorns. Curiosity, the first intellectual emotion of the child, the last of the old man—that is the ultimate base of epic and novel and tragedy alike.

> Yet all experience is an arch wherethro'
> Gleams that untravell'd world, whose margin fades
> For ever and for ever when I move.

Life is fascinating to watch, whatever it may be to experience. In *Iliad VII*, when Hector is about to challenge the Achaeans to single combat, Apollo and Athene perch in the shape of eagles on a great oak in the Trojan Plain, "delighting in the deeds of men"— the first of Greek tragic audiences. And so we too go to tragedies not in the least to get rid of emotions, but to have them more abundantly; to banquet, not to purge. Our lives are often dull; they are always brief in duration and confined in scope; but in drama or fiction, even the being "whose dull morrow cometh and is as to-day is" can experience, vicariously, something more. To be "tragic", however, the experience must have in addition a certain peculiar quality—"must", not for moral or philosophic reasons, but because if the experience were not of that kind, we should use a different word for it. Some other forms of art may be merely beautiful; by

73

Tragedy, I think, we imply also something fundamentally true to life. It need not be the whole truth, but it must be true. Twice at the theatre I can remember having felt in the midst of a play, "Yes, this is the very essence of Tragedy": once, in Turgenev's *A Month in the Country*, where the slow disillusionment of years is crowded into one agonized scene, and a girl frozen into a woman before our eyes. Were the truth and the beauty of it less perfect, we should feel it less keenly; were they less perfect, we might feel it more keenly than we could bear. As it is, we mutter, "How unbearable!——and yet, yes, that is how it happens, the inevitable change that comes on all of us, made visible here as never before. This is life. This is growing up. How appallingly—— how fascinatingly true!" And so again in the work of another Russian, *The Three Sisters* of Chekhov. A series of petty, futile disasters has passed across these women's lives; and now nothing is left them, not even (it might seem) anything tragic, only a monotony of hopelessness, like the flapping of burnt paper in an empty grate, as all that had lent meaning to their existence passes away from them with the music of the departing regiment——that music which goes marching on so gaily, so confidently, as if it at least had no part in these weary doubts, and knew whither it was going and why men are born. There is, for me, no more really tragic ending in all drama; for as we see these wasted figures stand before us, as we hear fife and bugle go dancing so light-heartedly upon their way, in that contrast seems embodied, for one eternal moment, the paradox of the tragedy of life, its hopefulness and its despair, its calling trumpets and its after silences. And here too the only consolation is the utter truthfulness: we have seen for an instant through its mists the sheer mountain-face of life.

So the essence of Tragedy reduces itself to this—the pleasure we take in a rendering of life both serious and true. It must be serious, whether or no it has incidentally comic relief. It must seem to matter, or else the experience would belong to a different category and need a different name. And it must also seem true, or it will not move us. This is all. It may be good for us, but that is not why we go to it. And watching scenes like those of Turgenev, the mind revolts with a sudden anger at the thought of the besetting narrowness of philosophers, who can so seldom be disinterested, who so often make life a reformatory, and beauty useful, and art a pill. Tragedy may teach us to live more wisely; but that is not why we go to it; we go to have the experience, not to use it.

But is there, beyond this, no definite attitude to life in general which we may call tragic, something in fact common to *The Oresteia* and *Othello*, *The Bacchæ* and *The Master Builder*, some common impression which they leave? Is there in tragedy something corresponding to that fundamental paradox of comedy, which men have seen supremely embodied in Falstaff—the eternal incongruity between the divine wit and the animal grossness of man? The answer is, I think, "Yes." And this paradox of Hamlet which answers that of Falstaff? It is the very same. "What a piece of work is a man!" cries the Tragic Muse; and Comedy echoes with a laugh, "What a piece of work!" Nietzsche's tragic antithesis seems nearer to the truth than his predecessors' simpler answers. For in Tragedy is embodied the eternal contradiction between man's weakness and his courage, his stupidity and his magnificence, his frailty and his strength. It is the transcendent commonplace of Pope:

> Placed on this isthmus of a middle state,
> A being darkly wise, and rudely great:
> With too much knowledge for the Sceptic side,
> With too much weakness for the Stoic's pride,
> He hangs between; in doubt to act, or rest,
> In doubt to deem himself a God, or Beast;
> In doubt his Mind or Body to prefer,
> Born but to die, and reas'ning but to err . . .
> Created half to rise, and half to fall:
> Great lord of all things, yet a prey to all;
> Sole judge of Truth, in endless Error hurl'd:
> The glory, jest, and riddle of the world!

That is the essential theme of Tragedy. The dramatist may be a pessimist like Euripides, or a Jansenist like Racine, or we know not what, like Shakespeare. There may a god out of a machine to come hereafter, a happy epilogue; but *Hamlet* or *Phèdre* call for neither of these; they need nothing to perfect them. They stand alone and we forget the rest—the after-life with its readjustments, the martyr's crown, the lost in their livery of flame. Here is a mirror held up to the fashion of this world; we can look in it and bear to look, without being turned to stone. Here the problem of evil and of suffering is set before us; often it is not answered, but always there is something that makes it endurable. It may be the thought that the hero, like Œdipus or Hamlet or Samson, has at last got nobly off the stage, away from the fitful fever of life.

> Vex not his ghost, O let him passe, he hates him
> That would upon the wracke of this tough world
> Stretch him out longer.

It may be simply the consolation of perfect language, as when Antigone passes with that last great cry down to her living tomb:

> O tomb, O bridal-chamber, prison-house
> Deep-delved, sure-guarded ever; whither I
> Pass and am gathered to my kin, all those
> Persephone has numbered with her dead!

It may be the sense that human splendour is greater and finer even in defeat than the blind universe that crushes it; as in the last cry of Synge's Deirdre— "It's a pitiful thing, Conchubor, you have done this night in Emain; yet a thing will be a joy and triumph to the ends of life and time."[1]

---

[1] Cf. the words of Hecuba at the close of the *Trojan Women* of Euripides:

> Had not God
> Turned upside-down the happiness of Troy.
> We should have lain forgot, instead of giving
> Songs to the poets of the after-time.

Or it may be simply the consolation of the sheer integrity which faces life as it is. The characters may no longer be heroes sublime even in their fall, they may be the ordinary men and women of Ibsen and Chekhov, over whose lack of tragic splendour critics have mourned so needlessly. Complaining of the want of great personalities in this play or that, they forgot the author. For the characters may be poor in spirit and feeble in desire, and the play remain tragic in spite of it, if we feel that the author is himself none of these things and has never cheated or paltered in his picture of men as they are. Tragedy, then, is a representation of human unhappiness which pleases us notwithstanding, by the truth with which it is seen and the fineness with which it is communicated —"l'amertume poignante et fortifiante de tout ce qui est vrai".

The world of everyday seems often a purposeless chaos, a mangy tiger without even the fearful symmetry of Blake's vision; but the world of tragedy we can face, for we feel a mind behind it and the symmetry is there. Tragedy, in fine, is man's answer to this universe that crushes him so pitilessly. Destiny scowls upon him: his answer is to sit down and paint her where she stands.

IV

THE ANCIENT CHORUS AND ITS MODERN COUNTERPARTS

IF this, then, is the end of Tragedy—so to portray life that its tears become a joy for ever—it remains to consider the various means by which this has been done from Æschylus to Ibsen.

Aristotle (*Poetics*, vi) finds in Tragedy six essential parts—Plot and Character; Diction and Ideas; the Lyrical or Musical element provided by the Chorus, and the Spectacular. And since, historically, Tragedy begins with song and dance, we may not inappropriately take first this musical element. It has indeed the additional interest of providing an excellent example of the way artistic evolution proceeds. For the Greek Chorus was not a mere luxury; it performed certain functions essential in any drama; and when it disappeared other means had to be found of doing its work. On the other hand it was the Chorus which also bequeathed to modern Europe that rule of the Three Unities which had ceased really to be essential once the Chorus itself had disappeared; yet for generations seemed so. And, lastly, its early predominance and subsequent extinction illustrate excellently that larger process which has been going on since time immemorial, off the stage as well as on it—the struggle of the Individual against the Group, of the One against the Many.

Tragedy begins with a dance of Anons. "Das Volk dichtet", it has been said of primitive poetry; here "das Volk tanzt". The individual hero and his heroic individuality are not yet. Exactly what sort of dance it was and what kind of ritual, has been and is a matter of violent controversy, which involves the meaning of the word "tragedy" itself.[1] But whatever the origin of the Chorus, the individual first made his dramatic appearance in the midst of this anonymous ritual when some innovator, Thespis it is said, about the middle of the sixth century B.C., had the idea of impersonating the various characters of the religious story which the dance celebrated, in the intervals while his dancers rested. So the first actor appeared. With Æschylus came a second, with Sophocles a third (giving new scope for tragic irony); and at this sacred number of three[2] Greek tragedy mysteriously stopped. With three actors on the stage a complicated drama can be performed, while a statuesque simplicity is still preserved.[3]

It is interesting to watch in the career of Æschylus himself how this battle of the individual with the group sways to and fro. In what *seems* his first extant play,[4] *The Suppliants*, we have a chorus of the fifty daughters of Danaus, the heroines of the piece:

[1] See p. 25, note 1.

[2] It is sometimes said that the *Œdipus at Colonus* of Sophocles is exceptional and requires four actors; but here, too, three will suffice. There was, of course, no restriction about employing "supers" in addition; it was the *speaking* parts that were limited.

[3] Further details in my *Greek Drama for Everyman*, 3-15.

[4] A recent papyrus fragment has cast doubt on this.

fleeing from the courtship of their fifty cousins, they invoke the protection of Argos and wrest this from its king by threatening suicide at his altars should he refuse. In *The Persians* (472 B.C.) the number fifty has been diminished to a more manageable twelve (increased later to fifteen): but these Persian elders, though thinned in numbers, remain august figures, full of the pomp and dignity of the gorgeous East and on equal terms with Queen Atossa herself; and when the ghost of King Darius rises like Samuel's at the end, he turns to them before addressing his Queen. All this is remote from Oriental servitude. In the next extant play, *The Seven against Thebes* (467), the Chorus no longer enters first; and when it appears, it consists of a shrieking throng of Theban women, who cower before the contemptuous reproaches of King Eteocles. In *Prometheus*[1] the nymphs of Ocean have still more clearly sunk to that position of powerless though sympathetic spectators, which is typical of most Greek Choruses; yet they show independence at the end and refuse, despite the menaces of Hermes, to forsake Prometheus when the earth opens to engulf him. In *Agamemnon* the degeneration of the Chorus as persons is almost complete; they have become the old men we know so well, the feeble onlookers who wring their hands in helplessness and beat vainly against bolted doors, while the murdering axe falls on the neck of the King of Kings; yet even they rally to defy the

---

[1] Belonging to the close of the poet's career; and by some dated after *The Oresteia* (*Agamemnon, Choephorœ, and Eumenides*) of 458.

usurper Ægisthus at the close. And now in the two plays that follow, the Chorus recovers for a final moment something of its ancient dignity. In *The Choephorœ* and *The Eumenides* it once more gives its name to the play; and in *The Eumenides* the old Æschylus seems to react towards the conventions of his youth and the Chorus rises once more to its supreme height in the figures of the avenging Furies. Yet the Furies in the end are defeated; and there is something very appropriate in their conversion by Athena into benign but shadowy figures of goodwill. For that is what the Chorus comes to be; until at last it fades like Echo, and becomes in Euripides at times a mere disembodied voice.

Conventions in Art are born rather than made: like most conventions the Greek Chorus is a beautiful accident, and like most accidents it is not perfect. Superbly as its great dramatists adapt and modify this relic of primitive religion to serve their art, just as Greek sculptors adapt their groups with an added beauty to the arbitrary triangle of the temple-pediment, there are times when we feel the Chorus an encumbrance and wish it away. On the other hand, the dramatists early realized how many important uses this standing stage-army could be made to serve. It can expound the past, comment on the present, forebode the future. It provides the poet with a mouthpiece and the spectator with a counterpart of himself. It forms a living foreground of common humanity above which the heroes tower; a living background of pure poetry which turns lamentation into music and horror into peace. It provides both a wall, as Schiller held, severing the drama like a magic circle from the real world, and a bridge between the heroic figures of legend and the average humanity of the audience. Thus while we await the returning Agamemnon, the elders of Argos sadly recall how in the past the maiden blood of Iphigeneia stained his departure for Troy. When Œdipus forgets the due self-restraint of a Hellene and a king, the elders of Thebes shake their heads in anxious disapproval. And while the bath of Clytemnestra still lies hidden in the future, long before the fatal moment arrives when that clinging purple mantle is to net the struggling king, the recurring idea of a net has haunted the lips of the Chorus, just as "the pistols of my father the General" are the refrain of *Hedda Gabler*, "the White Horses" the refrain of *Rosmersholm*. Beside the youthful courage of Antigone quaver in trembling contrast the old men of Thebes; from the convulsive passion of Phædra the vision of the women of Trœzen flees away to the untrodden caverns of the hills, to the careless freedom of the birds that pass cloud-like from land to land. When the miserable Pentheus is lured out, hypnotized, to disguise himself for his hideous death at his mother's hands, the thoughts of the Maenads escape to dream of their own happy revels in the lonely silence of the hills—

> Once again, until the dawning,
>   Shall I dance where feet flash white,
> While my face, flung back towards Heaven,

Drinks again the dews of night?—
As a fawn goes gaily leaping
　Where green meadows smile around,
When she has foiled the dreaded hunter,
　Breaking with a headlong bound
O'er the net where ambush lies,
While in vain the huntsman cries,
　Holloing on each rushing hound?
Swift as storm, by river pastures
　On she gallops, undismayed,
Glad of thickets no man knoweth,
Glad of green young life that groweth
　In the long-tressed woodland's shade.[1]

For this creation of atmosphere, of contrast, of escape and relief, the Greek Chorus in the hands of its masters is consummately used.

But the sure change comes. The choric odes that in Sophocles had retained the strict relevance of the music of opera, in Euripides tend (with Aristotle's disapproval) to resemble rather the merely diverting music of an *entr'acte*; in Agathon they have become completely disconnected, and the "Orchestra" is well on its way from its ancient sense—"the dancing-place of the chorus"—to its meaning in the theatre of our time. More and more this permanent stage crowd was felt to be a burden on the plot of the dramatist, as well as on the purse of the rich citizen who had to pay for it. The characters of Æschylus had been colossi, and even his choruses of heroic stature; the characters of Sophocles heroic, his

---

[1] *Bacchae*, 862-76; *Greek Drama for Everyman*, 329-30.

choruses simply human; the characters of Euripides become human, his choruses half ghosts. And finally the dead mummy of the chorus remains embalmed for ever in the neat summary of Horace[1]:

> An actor's part the chorus should sustain
> And do their best to get the plot in train:
> And whatsoe'er between the acts they chant
> Should all be apt, appropriate, relevant.
> Still let them give sage counsel, back the good,
> Attemper wrath, and cool impetuous blood,
> Praise the spare meal that pleases but not sates,
> Justice and law, and peace with unbarred gates,
> Conceal all secrets, and the gods implore
> To crush the proud and elevate the poor.

After this it is only its bare, dishevelled ghost that wails between the acts of the tragedies of Seneca. The Chorus that once had unified plays now serves to divide them into acts.

The ancient Chorus produced some of the finest passages in ancient literature; but also some of the flattest; its drawbacks have never been put more clearly—or gaily—than by Gray to Mason (1751)[2]: "A greater liberty in the choice of the fable, and the conduct of it, was the necessary consequence of re-trenching the Chorus. Love, and tenderness delight in privacy. The soft effusions of the soul, Mr Mason, will not bear the presence of a gaping, singing, dancing, moralizing, uninteresting crowd. And not love alone, but every passion is checked and cooled

---

[1] *Ars Poetica*, 193-201 (Conington's translation).
[2] *Correspondence* (ed. Toynbee and Whibley), I. 358.

by this fiddling crew. How could Macbeth and his wife have laid the design for Duncan's murder? What could they have said to each other in the Hall at midnight, not only if a chorus, but if a single mouse had been stirring there? Could Hamlet have met the Ghost, or taken his mother to task in *their* company? If Othello had said a harsh word to his wife before *them*, would they not have danced to the window, and called the watch? The ancients were perpetually confined and hampered by the necessity of using the Chorus, and, if they have done wonders notwithstanding this clog, sure I am they would have performed still greater wonders without it."

We come to the Middle Ages. From the tomb of Christ, as once perhaps of Dionysus, the drama rises again into life; again religious ritual becomes art. But no chorus reappears to dance down the cobbled streets of Coventry or Wakefield. The Middle Ages danced, even in the churchyard itself; but their dance failed to wed their drama. Only when the ancient world was rediscovered did the learned try to recapture the secret of its tragic chorus. But the choruses of their classical imitations, of *Gorboduc* and *Cornélie*, Fulke Greville and Ben Johnson, remain "vampire-cold". The decay of the classical chorus thus revived only repeated itself far more rapidly. After the first attempts to reproduce those Senecan choruses between the acts which preserved at all events some sort of relevance, we find Garnier writing candidly in the preface to his *Bradamante* (1580):

"Parce qu'il n'y a point de chœurs comme aux tragédies précédentes, pour la distinction des actes, celui qui voudroit faire réprésenter cette Bradamante, sera, s'il lui plaît, averti d'user d'entre-mêts, et les interposer entre les actes, pour ne les confondre, et ne mettre en continuation de propos ce qui requiert quelque distance du temps." The choric ode has thus already become again, as in Agathon, a mere interlude. Success lay, not in resurrecting the ancient convention, but in inventing other ways of doing what it had done. For if the popular Elizabethan playwright had no chorus, on the other hand he could have on the stage at once not three characters only, but almost as many as he chose. And a single one of these, like Enobarbus in *Antony and Cleopatra*, might suffice by himself to do much of the work the chorus once performed. Is the past to be recalled? Enobarbus will describe in poetry as vivid as an ode of Æschylus how Cleopatra first came to the arms of Antony.

> I will tell you.
> The Barge she sat in, like a burnisht Throne
> Burnt on the water: the Poope was beaten Gold,
> Purple the Sailes: and so perfumed that
> The Windes were Love-sicke with them. The Owers
>   were Silver,
> Which to the tune of Flutes kept stroke, and made
> The water which they beate, to follow faster,
> As amorous of their strokes. For her owne person,
> It beggered all description: she did lye
> In her Pavillion, cloth of Gold, of Tissue,

O'er-picturing that Venus, where we see
The fancie outworke Nature. On each side her
Stood pretty Dimpled Boyes, like smiling Cupids,
With divers-coulour'd Fannes whose winde did seem,
To glowe the delicate cheekes which they did coole,
And what they undid did.

Is comment needed on the present? Enobarbus will
reflect on the infatuation of his master.

I see men's Judgements are
A parcell of their Fortunes, and things outward
Do draw the inward quality after them
To suffer all alike—that he should dreame,
Knowing all measures, the full *Cæsar* will
Answer his emptinesse! *Cæsar*, thou hast subdu'de
His judgement too.

And if a hint of the future is required, Enobarbus
can forebode it.

If I were bound to Divine of this unity, I wold not
Prophesie so. . . . You shall find the bande that seemes to
tye their friendship together, will be the very strangler of
their Amity: *Octavia* is of a holy, cold, and still conversation
. . . he will to his Egyptian dish againe: then shall the sighes
of *Octavia* blow the fire up in *Cæsar*, and (as I said before)
that which is the strength of their Amity, shall prove the
immediate Author of their variance. *Anthony* will use his
affection where it is. Hee married but his occasion heere.

Where the Greek Chorus served as a foil, a type
of common humanity beside the heroic figures of
legend, the Shakespearian stage has its meaner

characters, its citizens, its crowds, its clowns. Where the Greek Chorus provided a lyric relief for tragic tension, Elizabethan dramatists have on the one hand the laughter of their fools, on the other the lyric beauty of their stage-songs and the poetry they can put in the mouth of almost any character, however sordid or villainous.

> All the Flowers of the Spring
> Meet to perfume our burying:
> These have but their growing prime,
> And man does flourish but his time.
> Survey our progresse from our birth,
> We are set, we grow, we turne to earth.
> Courts adieu, and all delights,
> All bewitching appetites;
> Sweetest Breath, and clearest eye,
> Like perfumes goe out and die;
> And consequently this is done
> As shadows wait upon the Sunne.

Such are the words which Webster chooses to put in the mouth of a swindling merchant (*The Devil's Law-Case*, v. 4).

The whole pace of the drama and its multiplicity of detail have increased tenfold. In passing from Sophocles to Shakespeare we seem to turn from the lonely mountain peak to the multitudinous whispers of the forest, from the Parthenon to the innumerable pinnacles of Gothic, from the grey simplicity of the pearl to the thousand facets of the diamond. In the rush of this new world there is only time to glimpse things for a moment as they flash by. Where

Dejanira or Polyxena had a whole ode of lamentation
for her fate. Desdemona has but her brief Willow-
song; Imogen, Fidele's dirge; Ophelia, her heart-
broken snatches of madness. Where Œdipus was
warned by the wise deliberations of his Elders, Lear
has but the sudden piping of the fool—

> Then they for sodaine joy did weepe,
> And I for sorrow sung,
> That such a King should play bo-peepe,
> And goe the Fooles among.

Where the old men of Argos slowly unburdened
their hearts of dark presentiment, in *Richard III*
"Enter Three Citizens." In *Hamlet*, again, the work
of the ancient Chorus is divided between Horatio,
and the gravediggers, and Fortinbras with his
healthy commonplaces, and, above all, Hamlet himself, whose "To be or not to be?" might be a chorus
of Euripides, just as his "What a piece of work is a
man!" actually answers to one of Sophocles. In the
obvious difference of the means employed, this
underlying likeness, this long continuity in the
development of the drama, is not always seen.

Since the Elizabethans, however, Tragedy, where
it has succeeded at all, has tended to become ever less
lyrical and less poetic. The French neo-classic stage
austerely denied its audience any lyrical relief; the
service of providing both the exposition of the plot
and examples of average humanity was left to its
confidants. And in modern tragedy the lyric element
may either disappear altogether as in *Ghosts*, or

pervade a whole play as in *La Città Morta* or *Riders to the Sea*. To-day the main characters are themselves ordinary human beings; therefore they do not need ordinary human beings to contrast with them. And yet even now in curious, isolated figures like Dr Relling and Father Keegan, or the old servants in *Rosmersholm* and *The Cherry Orchard*, we may, if we care, see the disinherited descendants of those who once moved so proudly around Tantalid and Labdacid beneath Athena's hill.

The Chorus is dead. Its music has fallen to opera, that "*beau monstre*"; and even its poetry finds only fitful utterance on the lips of the dwellers in this modern world which sometimes, indeed, still loves poetry, but seldoms succeeds in living it.

V

PLOT

OF the Plot of Tragedy Aristotle makes three general
observations: that it must be of a certain size (vi. 2);
that it must be of a certain structure (vii. 2-3); and
that it is the most important thing—"the soul"—of
drama (vi. 9-15).

Its size is obviously limited, because it must on
the one hand be long enough for the catastrophe to
occur, and on the other hand short enough to be
grasped as a single artistic whole, and not (an un-
usual flight of fancy for Aristotle) "like a creature[1] a
thousand miles long". In practice, on the European
stage, this has meant a usual length of from two to
three hours. The drama has generally been less liable
to capricious extravagances and whimsies of fashion
than other forms of literature, just as architecture has
been less liable to them than the other visual arts;
simply because it is too expensive. Artists, or those
who finance them, are inevitably more cautious
where there is a risk of wasting not merely a few
sheets of paper or feet of canvas, but a whole troop

[1] Or possibly "a picture".

of actors or tons of wood and stone. And so the acting drama has suffered less both from other vagaries and from that elephantiasis which has occasionally afflicted the epic and the novel. The limits set by the logic of Aristotle, and by the capacity of the ordinary human being to sit still, remain decisive; and though this capacity varies to some extent in different times and countries, no more need be said.

Of the structure of tragedy Aristotle has observed, with his usual fine disregard of apparent platitude, that it must have a beginning, a middle, and an end.[1] A "beginning" is a situation which has definite consequences, though not very obvious causes; a "middle" is a situation with both causes and consequences; and an "end" is the result of the "middle", but creates no further situation in its turn. Taken literally, since every event has both causes and consequences, this would mean that dramas must last for eternity; but though they may sometimes seem to, this is not Aristotle's intention. Events tend to occur in clusters. A volcano, even when continuously active, has eruptions which form episodes complete in themselves; and the events of a tragedy are like such an eruption. All that Aristotle is insisting upon is that a play should have good and obvious reasons for beginning where it begins, and for ending where it ends; and that its incidents should follow from one another by a clear chain of causation, without coincidence and without irrelevance. There shall

[1] Contrast **Chekhov**: "Stories should have neither a beginning nor an end."

be nothing which is not clearly caused by what precedes, nothing which is not clearly the cause of what follows. (Compare Johnson's objection to the episodic nature of *Samson Agonistes*.) On the stage of Aristotle no miser "leans against the wall and grows generous"; no British troops arrive by chance to the rescue in the nick of time. On the other hand we shall not have Falstaff. For what is he but a magnificent irrelevance in a play about Henry IV? And Falstaff may well seem a heavy price to pay for logic.

Why should logical causation seem thus important in drama? Partly, I take it, for artistic reasons. Art seems often a combination of two human impulses— our fondness for reproducing life, and our fondness for design, pattern, order. So we like the design of a plot to seem inevitable—to have both a plan that seems causally inevitable, and a pattern that seems artistically inevitable.

But why should we so want it to seem causally inevitable? In real life, on the contrary, we are often less fascinated by the probable than by the wildly improbable. It was not just the loss of life on the *Titanic* that moved the world—it was the uncanny coincidence that, against incalculable odds, brought together the great ship, on her maiden voyage, from the east and the iceberg from the unimaginable remoteness of the north. That a notebook written by Napoleon in his young days as officer of artillery should close with the entry "Sainte-Hélène, petite île" is enthralling because its tragic irony seems incredible. But in a Napoleonic play it might well fail with the audience—not knowing it true, they might reject it as far-fetched and artificial.

Why this difference? Because, I take it, in life, knowing it real, we are enthralled by its becoming fantastic: but with drama, knowing it unreal, we need to believe it real, before we can enjoy its strangeness. We do not feel all the time that a play is just a play (here Johnson exaggerated); we do not all the time suspend our disbelief (here Coleridge exaggerated); we hover to and fro between the two—like a bather intermittently touching bottom with his toes. The spectator does not rush to rescue Desdemona, for at a lower level of consciousness he remains aware she is an actress; but the illusion may be strong enough to draw tears.[1] Yet this valued illusion is fragile. A false note, a jarring improbability—and at once the magic carpet crashes. "*Incredulus odi*"—"I disbelieve, and I hate it." Hence the truth of Aristotle's dictum (xxiv. 10, xxv. 17) that a plausible impossibility is preferable to an unplausible possibility[2]. (Better, for instance, Caliban than Sir Charles

[1] With simpler minds it can, of course, be stronger. In a Chinese market-town in 1678 the actor who played the treacherous Ch'in Kuei was so good that a spectator leapt on the stage and stabbed him fatally. Similarly intense emotions seem to have been sometimes aroused by medieval drama.

[2] Cf. Oscar Wilde on R. L. Stevenson: "There is such a thing as robbing a story of its reality by trying to make it too true, and *The Black Arrow* is so inartistic as not to contain a single anachronism to boast of, while the transformation of Dr Jekyll reads dangerously like an experiment out of *The Lancet*."

Grandison.) So with play or novel as a whole; a beautifully forged chain of causation is not only a positive aesthetic pleasure, it is also important to prevent our being jarred, resentfully, from our dream.

However, this is no place for a detailed history of logic on the stage. The Greeks, with that strange, precocious, instinctive artistry they so often show, practised it long before Aristotle was born to make it into a theory; the Elizabethans ignored it—in a few happy instances with triumphant success—often, disastrously; the French learnt it from the ancients, and so redoubled its rigour that in such matters La Harpe's little finger is thicker than Aristotle's loins; while finally the modern drama has lost the innocence of the Elizabethans, so that a play as rambling as, say, *The Winter's Tale* would probably seem a monstrosity to-day, and Ibsen returns to an almost Greek severity of form; though on the other hand we have finally abandoned the extremer pedantries of neoclassicism in its stress on "unity".

But to return to Aristotle's "beginning"; we have seen that these apparently elementary statements of his are apt to lend themselves to interpretations as startlingly diverse as the provisions of a simple-seeming will and testament. What is, in fact, the beginning of the tragedy of Œdipus? To Sophocles, the coming of that oracle about the plague, which like a cold breath lifts the corner of the veil that hides the past of Œdipus and his wife Jocasta. And so we have that marvel of construction, *Œdipus*

Tyrannus; which may be rudely anatomized as follows[1]:

ACT I. The arrival of an oracle about the plague in Thebes, commanding the banishment of the unknown murderer of the late King Laïus.

ACT II. Investigating the murder, Œdipus, quick-tempered and suspicious, quarrels with Tiresias, the true servant of the gods.

ACT III. He quarrels likewise with Creon, the true servant of the State.

ACT IV. A Messenger comes from Corinth; Jocasta realizes the truth and goes out to hang herself; while Œdipus, misunderstanding all, persists in his inquiry, and the Chorus rashly exults in the hope of discovering that some great, perhaps divine, parentage is his.

ACT V. Owing to the revelations of the Messenger a Herdsman is brought from Cithæron. Œdipus in his turn realizes the truth—that he is the son of Laïus and Jocasta—and rushes out to blind himself.

---

[1] Greek tragedies were not, of course, divided into Acts: their subdivisions are named with reference to the once all-important Chorus, thus (cf. *Poetics*, xii):

PROLOGOS: the part before the entrance of the Chorus.

PARODOS: entrance-song of Chorus.

EPEISODION: interval between songs of the Chorus; the counterpart (together with the Prologos and Exodos) of our Acts. Their number is not fixed; though by the time of Horace (*Ars Poetica*, 189) who drew on Hellenistic criticism, the sacred number of five Acts has appeared; and this is observed by Seneca.

STASIMON: song of the Chorus. The number of these varies with that of the Epeisodia they separate.

EXODOS: all after the last song of the Chorus.

Act VI. Another Messenger announces the self-murder of Jocasta and the self-blinding of Œdipus, who enters and laments his fate, and is then driven into banishment.

Now, had Ibsen treated this story, he would probably have chosen to cover, however differently, the same events, except that he would have ended with Act V; and, being Philistine enough to find the lamentations of Œdipus in Act VI a little tedious, I should not regret it. But had Shakespeare treated the subject, we may imagine a scheme like this (recalling at moments *The Winter's Tale*):

Act I. The oracle comes to Laïus, King of Thebes, warning him that if he begets a son he will die by that son's hand.

The child Œdipus is born, exposed on Cithæron (like Perdita on the coast of Bohemia), and carried off to Corinth.

Act II. Œdipus, grown to manhood, visits Delphi to inquire his parentage. The god tells him that he will kill his father and marry his mother. Fleeing from his destiny, he meets King Laïus on the road and kills him, not knowing who he is.

Act III. He encounters the Sphinx on her mountain above Thebes, answers her riddle, and so delivers the city from her ravages. In return he is made king and weds Queen Jocasta.

Acts IV-V. These might cover the same ground as the whole play of Sophocles, though ending, like Ibsen, more abruptly and without the long final lamentation.

This may illustrate the differences between the classic and romantic approaches to a story. It will be seen that the romantic method is not without its advantages; and one may regret that Shakespeare did not handle this superb legend instead of some of the puerile plots on which he too often wasted his genius. Only imagine what he might have made of some of its scenes! For if the romantic form has a less perfect and close-knit unity, it gains on the other hand a far greater variety of dramatic episodes to choose from. It is free, too, from that forced artificiality which may result from having to squeeze the whole action into a dozen hours; and it is certainly better to strain the spectator's imagination than the facts of life. Lastly, it leaves time for growth of character.

And yet in spite of this the modern dramatist seldom takes these Elizabethan liberties with time and place. The fascination of form has grown stronger; in spreading the action over years we feel that the intensity of drama may be weakened, and the magic cauldron go off the boil. Let too many years pass over a person's head and he is no longer quite the same person. Further, in tragedy a terrible inevitability is gained by beginning, not at the very beginning, but just before the catastrophe, when the tragic mistakes have been made and are beyond God Himself to undo; for then

> All things are taken from us and become
> Portions and parcels of the dreadful past.

The past indeed is the most tragic of the tenses. If it was happy, it is no more; if it was disastrous, it cannot be undone. And so, while the Unities of Time and Place ceased to be essential with the disappearance of the Chorus (although it was centuries before this simple truth was seen), modern tragedy has learnt to use moderation in transgressing them, particularly the Unity of Time.

Of all the various ways of beginning there is no space to speak at length. But it will repay the curious to study comparatively the differing habits of the dramatists—Æschylus' great opening monologues (after his two first extant plays which begin with the chorus); the quieter dialogue between two characters common in Sophocles, who had increased the actors to three and so could better afford to begin with two of them on the stage; the often pallid and artificial prologues of Euripides, sacrificing artistic illusion to a naked clarity[1]; the prologizing ghosts of Seneca, loved and copied by the Renaissance; and Shakespeare's method of quiet conversations followed almost at once by some sudden excitement.[2] Beginnings can of course be loud as well as quiet. Of the opening with a crash there is a superb example in Webster's *White Devil*—"Banisht!" But the quieter type tends to prevail. It is rash to sprint at the start of a five-mile race. And the unpunctuality of the public may make the first speeches inaudible.

---

[1] The prologue of *Hippolytus*, like that of Shakespeare's *Troilus and Cressida*, seems to me a splendid exception.

[2] So in *Romeo and Juliet*, *Hamlet*, *Macbeth*, *Othello*, and *King Lear*.

After beginning his plot, however, the next thing for the dramatist is to explain it. And here a progressive growth of technical skill has been maintained right down to our own day. The Greek audience knew many of the heroic legends, at least roughly, beforehand[1]; and the Greek dramatist was helped to some extent by having a chorus which could recall antecedent events in its lyrics. The Elizabethans, on the other hand, beginning at the very beginning, had less to explain; and it is noticeable that when Shakespeare is for once really faced with the problem in *The Tempest*, where he almost adopts the Unities, how incompetently he manages it.[2] We little wonder that Miranda goes to sleep; and when Prospero turns and continues his exposition to Ariel, we have only too good an example of that familiar clumsiness by which one character is made to repeat to another

---

[1] The *Poetics* does indeed say (ix. 8), "There is no need to cling wholly to the traditional legends. That would be an absurd attempt; *for even the known stories are known only to few.*" But there seems something wrong here. Aristotle's contemporary, Antiphanes the comic poet (*c.* 388-*c.* 311), complains on the contrary that tragic poets have an enviable advantage over comic in that their plots are already familiar to the audience without need of explanation (fr. 191). Aristophanes (*c.* 450-*c.* 385) is full of mythological allusions; Menander (*c.* 342-*c.* 290) puts them in the mouth even of a realistic rustic. Poetry played a large part in Athenian education; even a few years' attendance in the theatre would familiarize many of the stories. We know, for example, of 12 plays on Œdipus, 7 on Medea, 7 on Philoctetes. I suspect that Greek spectators knew many heroic legends as well as English readers *used* to know Biblical ones. (Modern ignorance of these may well dismay even the sceptic.)

[2] It is strange to me that Coleridge gave this exposition his particular admiration.

what both know, merely for the benefit of the audience.

> *Prospero.*   Hast thou forgot
> The fowle Witch *Sycorax*, who with Age and Envy
> Was growne into a hoope? Hast thou forgot her?
>
> *Ariel.* No, Sir.
>
> *Pro.* Thou hast: where was she born? speak: tell me.
>
> *Ar.* Sir, in *Argier.*
>
> *Pro.* Oh, was she so? I must
> Once in a moneth recount what thou hast bin,
> Which thou forget'st. This damn'd Witch *Sycorax*,
> For mischiefes manifold, and sorceries terrible
> To enter humane hearing, from *Argier*,
> Thou know'st, was banished; for one thing she did
> They would not take her life: is not this true?
>
> *Ar.* I, Sir.
>
> *Pro.* This blew-ey'd hag was hither brought with child,
> And here was left by th' Saylors . . .
>   Then was this Island,
> (Save for the Son that she did littour heere,
> A frekelld whelpe, hag-borne) not honour'd with
> A humane shape.
>
> *Ar.* Yes: *Caliban* her sonne.
>
> *Pro.* Dull thing, I say so; he, that *Caliban*,
> Whom now I keepe in service.

The reader of this may excusably be reminded by its too obvious artifice of a passage in that play of Sheridan's which so well and gaily earns its title of *The Critic* (ii. 2):

Sir Walter Raleigh. Thy fears are just.

Sir Christopher Hatton. But where? whence? when? and what
The danger is—methinks I fain would learn.

Sir Walt. You know, my friend, scarce two revolving suns
And three revolving moons have closed their course,
Since haughty Philip, in despite of peace,
With hostile hand hath struck at England's trade.

Sir Christ. I know it well.

Sir Walt. Philip, you know, is proud Iberia's king!

Sir Christ. He is.

Sir Walt. His subjects in base bigotry
And Catholic oppression held,—while we,
You know, the Protestant persuasion hold.

Sir Christ. We do.

Sir Walt. You know, beside, his boasted armament,
The famed Armada, by the Pope baptized,
With purpose to invade these realms—

Sir Christ.   Is sailed,
Our last advices so report. . . .

Dangle. Mr Puff, as he *knows* all this, why does Sir Walter go on telling him?

Puff. But the audience are not supposed to know anything of the matter, are they?

Sneer. True; but I think you manage ill: for there certainly appears no reason why Sir Walter should be so communicative.

Puff. 'Fore God, now, that's one of the most ungrateful observations I ever heard!—for the less inducement he has to tell all this, the more, I think, you ought to be obliged to him; for I'm sure you'd know nothing of the matter without it.

The French neo-classic stage managed fairly efficiently with the help of its serviceable, though wooden, confidants. But it is in the last hundred years, with the disappearance of the soliloquy, and the growing sensitiveness of audiences to anything improbable, that this problem has become really difficult, and its handling an art in itself.

Clearly the exposition must itself be dramatic, or it will both be a bore and seem an excrescence. To be dramatic it must be charged with emotion: for a *résumé* of the bare facts can hardly be thrilling in itself. Here it is fascinating to watch the growth of Ibsen's skill, replacing the hackneyed use of confidants, or of servants who talk about their mistresses as they lay the table, by the mastery which in *The Master Builder* or *Ghosts* or *Rosmersholm* makes the exposition become one agonized confession. The situation is not only revealed: the revelation in itself assures and hastens the catastrophe. These tortured souls tell their tale despite themselves, like the damned before Dante's Minos; their situation makes it impossible for them to be silent; and their speaking brings their ruin.

But there is another important question connected with this. Exactly how much is to be explained beforehand, how much to be kept secret from the audience? At first, surprise seems one of the dramatist's most obvious and brilliant weapons. Says Lope de Vega: "Keep your secret to the end. The audience will turn their faces to the door and their backs to the stage when there is no more to learn." Similarly Boileau (*Art Poétique*, iii.):

L'esprit ne se sent pas plus vivement frappé
Que lorsqu'en un sujet d'intrigue enveloppé
D'un secret tout à coup la vérité connue
Change tout, donne à tout une face imprévue.

And so ingenious critics have been found to wish
that when Hamlet stabs Polonius behind the arras,
Shakespeare had concealed the victim's identity and
allowed his audience, like his hero, to think for a
moment that it was the King; and to regret, again,
that in the Screen-scene of *The School for Scandal* the
audience is not left as ignorant as Sir Peter Teazle,
who it was behind the screen. Indeed, ingenious
managers have been known to do their best to improve Sheridan by at all events burning red fire in
the wings at the fatal moment when the screen is
overturned. Perhaps we may begin to wonder after
all this whether surprise is really so valuable an
engine. The Greeks managed with very little, for with
them the course of the story was known. Dryden has
described in his witty, exaggerated way how the
Athenian audience, as soon as the name of Œdipus
was uttered, knew all that was to follow—his murder
of his father and his marriage with his mother and
the rest of it, and "sat with a kind of yawning expectation till he was to come with his eyes pulled out,
and speak a hundred or two verses in a tragic tone in
complaint of his misfortune". Yet this was not so
serious a deprivation as might seem; for after all,
once we have seen it, the story of the newest play is
known. Surprise is for one night, not for all time.
The dramatist who snatches at it is liable to pluck

the blossom and lose the fruit. Even when it succeeds it may be too successful, and leave the audience too astonished to give their full attention to what immediately follows. Surprise may, in general, be left to melodrama and some kinds of comedy: Tragedy has in her quiver two more keenly pointed shafts than this—Suspense and Tragic Irony.

From both we get an effect which is not exhausted in a flash, and which is not staled by age. To the nervous person in the inn it is not the shoe dropped carelessly in the next room that is a source of agony, but the suspense of waiting for the second shoe to drop. And it is the power to create the tense, over-charged atmosphere before the storm, to "pile the dim outlines of the coming doom", that forms no small part of the impressiveness of Æschylus or Webster, or, in a different way, of Ibsen. The *leitmotiv* of the fatal net in the *Agamemnon*, the recurrent playing on the white horses of Rosmersholm, are but methods of working on the nerves of an audience; and in more obvious ways most dramatists have used this weapon of suspense. The Ghost in *Hamlet* is long talked of before it appears; Tartuffe is kept back until Act III; we hear the caged pacing overhead of John Gabriel Borkman long before he is disclosed to our expectant eyes. To return for a moment to Sheridan—

Sneer. But, pray, is not Queen Elizabeth to appear?

Puff. No, not once—but she is to be talked of for ever; so that, egad, you'll think a hundred times that she is on the point of coming in.

Sneer. Hang it, I think it's a pity to keep *her* in the green room all the night.

Puff. Oh no, that always has a fine effect—it keeps up expectation.

Of course, where surprise effects are greatly conceived, they may continue to be effective as suspense effects, even when they have ceased to surprise; like the cry in *Little Eyolf*—"the crutch is floating!"— "krykken flyder"—or the death-blow of Othello:

> I pray you in your Letters,
> When you shall these unluckie deeds relate
> Speake of me, as I am. Nothing extenuate,
> Nor set downe ought in malice.
> Then must you speake
> Of one that lov'd not wisely, but too well;
> Of one, not easily Iealous, but being wrought,
> Perplexed in the extreame: Of one, whose hand
> (Like the base Indian) threw a Pearle away,
> Richer than all his Tribe. . . . Set you downe this:
> And say, besides, that in *Aleppo* once,
> Where a malignant, and a Turban'd Turke
> Beate a Venetian, and traduc'd the State,
> I tooke by th' throat the circumcised Dogge,
> And smoate him, thus. (*He stabs himself.*)

Tragic Irony, again, demands full knowledge in the audience, though for the character such irony may be either conscious or unconscious. That is, the speaker may be intentionally ironical; or the audience alone may see a double meaning (though sometimes only retrospectively) in what is spoken by a character with no *arrière pensée* at all. And as words may be ironic, so may actions and events. In the age of Thomas Hardy, of *Satires of Circumstances*, *Life's Little Ironies*, and *Time's Laughing-Stocks*, we hardly need instances of this. But in the close of the *Electra* of Sophocles is so elaborate an example of these four kinds of irony, conscious and unconscious, in word and in deed, that it may be quoted here. Orestes with his friend Pylades, returning in disguise to Argos with a false message of his own death, has already killed his mother Clytemnestra in revenge for her murder of his father. Her paramour and accomplice Ægisthus now arrives from the country, eager to learn from the "strangers'" own lips the glad tidings that the dreaded Orestes is dead. He enters and finds Electra standing at his palace-door (*Electra*, 1450 ff.).

Ægisthus. Where shall I find these strangers? Tell me quickly.

Electra (pointing to the palace-door).

There—they have touched their hostess to the heart.

Æg. Is it true, that they bring news of Orestes' death?

El. They have brought Orestes' self along with them.

Æg. What, is he here, for my own eyes to see?

El. Ay, here indeed—and yet a grisly sight.

Æg. For once you bring me joy—it is little like you!

El. I wish you joy, if joy it brings indeed.

Æg. Ho, silence there! fling wide our palace-doors—

(The doors open, revealing the disguised figures of Orestes and Pylades standing beside the shrouded body of Clytemnestra on a bier. Ægisthus goes up to it.)

For Argos and Mycenæ to behold;

So that all such as have lived hitherto
On idle hopes of this Orestes here,
Now seeing him dead, kick at my curb no more
Nor court my righteous wrath to teach them wisdom. . . .
Unveil the face, that one so near and dear
May have from me his due of lamentation.

   Orestes. Unveil it thou. This is thy part, not mine,
To see what lies there and to call it dear.

   Æg. Thou sayest well. I will. But quickly now,
Call Clytemnestra, if she is within.

   Or. She is beside thee. Look nowhere else for her.

   Æg. (lifting the face-cloth from the face). O God, what sight
    is this!

   Or. Afraid? Is that face so strange?

Here, surely, are compensations for the short-
lived pleasures of surprise. The great dramatists,
then, have learned as a rule not so much to startle
their audiences as to take them into their confidence.
If the gods alone, as the adage says, can be spectators
in the world, the spectators in the world of the theatre
should often be as gods, knowing all or almost all.
Against de Vega and Boileau we may set the homely
common sense of Anthony Trollope: "The author
and the reader should move along in full confidence
with each other. Let the personages of the drama
undergo for us a complete Comedy of Errors among
themselves, but let the spectator never mistake the
Syracusan for the Ephesian." The detective play or
novel provides exceptions to this; but they are hardly
the highest types of fiction or drama.

So far we have briefly discussed the ways of opening the tragic plot and of explaining it, and how far that exposition should leave room for surprise, or, on the contrary, cultivate suspense and irony. But on this last point more remains to be said. Of tragic irony in its familiar forms Aristotle has said nothing, but of that form of tragedy where the whole plot is itself built on the irony of fate, where the engineer is hoisted with his own petard, and the very means which should bring safety brings only ruin, or what was meant to destroy, on the contrary, preserves—of this Aristotle has said a great deal, which has often been misunderstood even by his standard commentators. And as this is perhaps the most penetrating thing Aristotle has to say of the tragic plot at all, and is essentially connected with his famous doctrine of the Tragic Error, it is worth clearing up even at some length.

The most moving things in tragedy, Aristotle observes (vi. 13), are "*peripeteia* and *anagnorisis*". It is usual to render these two words "reversal and recognition"; and both renderings seem to me misleading. The only reason for translating *peripeteia* by "reversal of fortune" is that it bears this sense in later Greek and in the modern languages which have adopted the word. In this latter sense it is a *peripeteia* when Job's long prosperity is destroyed, or the long victorious Germans hurled back from El Alamein. But a very little study either of the drama, or of Aristotle, would surely suggest that this sense of *peripeteia* makes nonsense of Aristotle. He implies, for example (xxiv. 1-2), that there are no *peripeteias* in the *Iliad*: yet it is full of changes of fortune. There is no space here to go into the linguistic evidence[1]; but that is really hardly necessary, seeing that Aristotle has himself given a perfectly lucid explanation of what he means (xi. 1), which may be paraphrased as follows: "A *peripeteia* occurs when a course of action intended to produce a result x, produces the reverse of x. Thus the messenger from Corinth tries to cheer Œdipus and dispel his fear of marrying his mother; but by revealing who Œdipus really is, he produces exactly the opposite result. Again, in *Lynceus* the hero of that name is led off to execution, while Danaus goes with him as his intending murderer; but the upshot is that Lynceus escapes, while Danaus is killed himself."[2]

And is this, it will be asked, the most moving constituent of tragedy? We might think that Aristotle was here deserting the obvious for the absurd; yet his dictum is not so eccentric as it seems.

[1] The true rendering was first established by Vahlen in 1866. For a detailed discussion of the question see an article by the present writer in *The Classical Review* for Aug.-Sept. 1923.

[2] As told by Æschylus in his *Suppliants*, the fifty sons of Aegyptus pursued and forcibly wedded their fifty cousins, the daughters of Danaus, in the land of Argos. But on the bridal-night these rough wooers were murdered by their brides, at the command of Danaus— all except Lynceus, who was loved and spared by his wife Hypermestra, "*splendide mendax*". In the play here referred to (by Theodectes, *c.* 375-334, a pupil of Plato and Aristotle) it would seem that after Hypermestra had lived some time by stealth with her husband, and borne him a son, Lynceus was discovered and ordered by Danaus, now King of Argos, to execution. But the Argives rose against the bloodthirsty old monarch, killed him, and made Lynceus and Hypermestra their king and queen instead.

In the *peripeteia*, rightly understood, is implied a whole tragic philosophy of life; and in the practice of tragedy, once we see the true meaning of the term, we shall discover with what amazing frequency the thing itself recurs. For the deepest tragedy is not when men are struck down by the blow of chance or fate, like Job, or Maurya in *Riders to the Sea*; nor yet when they are destroyed by their enemies, like Polyxena, or Henry VI; but when their destruction is the work of those that wish them well, or of their own unwitting hands. For it is the perpetual tragic irony of the Tragedy of Life that again and again men do thus laboriously contrive their own annihilation, or kill the thing they love. When Dejanira, sending her husband the love-philtre which was to win him back, poisons him, so that he dies cursing her; when Œdipus runs headlong into the jaws of the very destiny from which he flees; when Barabas falls into his own boiling cauldron, or Shylock is caught in his own bond; when Othello at last sees himself as one who has flung away, like an ignorant savage, the priceless jewel of his own happiness; when Macbeth is lured by the equivocations of the devil to make his own perdition sure; when Lear delivers himself into the hands of the two daughters that despise him, and rejects the only one that loves—all these are *peripeteias* in the true sense of Aristotle—what Horatio calls "purposes mistook, Fallen on the inventors' heads". For the most poignant tragedy of human life is the work of human blindness—the Tragedy of Errors.

In tragic life, God wot,
No villain need be. Passions spin the plot:
We are betrayed by what is false within.

In vain men pray, like Ajax on the plains of Troy, at
least to perish in the light and seeing the faces of
their foes; they fall blindly in the fatal confusion of a
world "where ignorant armies clash by night". This,
indeed, is in a sense the oldest as well as the deepest
tragedy on earth—the tragedy of our First Parents,
who plucked the apple in the hope that they should
live as gods, and "knew not eating death". The beasts
perish by enemies or by disease; it is the privilege
of man alone, in his foolish, blinded cunning, to
dig his own grave. This is the irony of Juvenal—

Magnaque numinibus vota exaudita malignis.
Petitions granted by malignant gods,
And prayers on which a bitter heaven smiles.

And in yet another form it is the crowning paradox
of Christ: "Whosoever will save his life, shall lose it."

Now, once it is seen that by his *peripeteia* Aristotle
means this tragic effect of human effort producing
exactly the opposite result to its intention, this irony
of human blindness, we see at last why he connects
the *peripeteia* so closely with the *anagnorisis* or "discovery".[1] The *peripeteia*, in short, is the working in

[1] "Recognition" is a mistranslation. We associate the word too
closely with the narrow sense of discovering a *person's* identity;
whereas *anagnorisis* may equally well signify the discovery of *things*
unknown before, and applies alike to the recognition of Imogen by
Posthumus and the realization by Othello of the true facts of his
own tragedy. An *anagnorisis* is a recognition of a truth—that person
A is A, or that proposition p is the case.

blindness to one's own defeat: the *anagnorisis* is the realization of the truth, the opening of the eyes, the sudden lightning-flash in the darkness.

> Then there came
> On that blind sin swift eyesight like a flame.

This flash of revelation may appear, as Aristotle points out, either before it is too late, or after; before, as in the *Cresphontes* of Euripides, where the mother with uplifted weapon realizes just in time that the supposed murderer of her son, asleep before her, is that son himself; or as the summer lightning revealed to David Balfour at the vital moment that abyss before his feet on the ruined staircase of the House of Shaws. In such cases there is, of course, a happy ending. Or the flash may come after the catastrophe, serving only to reveal it and complete it, as when Œdipus discovers his guilt, or Rustum or Cuchulain recognizes the dying son he has himself slain.

Turn to modern drama: the *peripeteia* and "discovery" still keep their central place. In Ibsen's *Doll's House* Nora, trying to save her husband, thereby loses him; and the ensuing cry of recognition rings clear in her own words: "It burst upon me that I had been living here these eight years with a strange man." In consequence, she herself abandons the husband she has been struggling so desperately to keep. The *peripeteia* is complete.

Thus, though Aristotle says nothing of tragic irony as such, he makes this particular irony of circumstances the crucial thing in tragedy in general and the very basis of its classification. For he divides tragedies (x. 1-2) into two classes, "simple" and "complex"—those that have *peripeteia* or *anagnorisis* and those that have not—Tragedies of Error, we might say, as against the far rarer and on the whole less significant Tragedies of Simple Circumstance, like *The Trojan Women* of Euripides. We may, indeed, definitely summarize the two kinds of tragedy in the words of two different passages of *Lear*:

> As Flies to wanton Boyes, are we to th' Gods—
> They kill us for their sport.

That is Aristotle's "simple" tragedy of circumstance. But again:

> The Gods are just, and of our pleasant vices
> Make instruments to plague us.

There we have the "complex" tragedy of recoil, with its *peripeteia*; and we may be reminded of Hegel's statement of the same principle: "The character that is dramatic plucks for himself the fruit of his own deeds."

Yet it must be recognized also that the vice by which men are "plagued" may sometimes be simply that natural human weakness which is unable to foresee the future. And here we come to the other famous Aristotelian doctrine of the ἁμαρτία (*hamartia*) or Tragic Error. This too has been curiously misunderstood, and in consequence the connection between the Tragedy of Errors with its *peripeteia*

(xi) and this Tragic Error (xiii—for xii is probably an interpolation) was wholly blurred, while the meaning of *peripeteia* was itself misrepresented; whereas it now becomes clear why Aristotle passes from considering the Tragedy of Errors to discussing the Tragic Error. For the word he uses means simply "a mistake", though there have always been persistent attempts on the part of moralizing critics to make the *hamartia* much more definitely a moral weakness, a sin, than it really is. For poetic justice has always been dear to the mediocre mind, and sometimes to minds not mediocre. It is so satisfactory to the complacency of prosperous persons to insist that those less fortunate are so only by their own fault, and that those on whom the Tower of Siloam fell somehow deserved it. And it has been all the easier to make this mistake, because Aristotle himself seems slightly confused between what is ethically good and what is æsthetically good, or magnificent. That confusion was naturally easier for the Greek, who used the same adjective (καλός) to describe a "good" thing and a "beautiful" one, and had no belief in the goodness of such unmagnificent qualities as meekness and humility. We shall find the same muddle between ethic and æsthetic goodness, between virtue and splendour of character, appearing again later in Aristotle's demand that the characters of tragedy must be good or fine (χρηστά). For a race so abundantly intellectual as to produce the Socratic dogma "Virtue *is* Knowledge", it was easy to obscure the difference between error and sin. Greek philosophy indeed was curiously prone to forget the weakness of the human will. But the important thing here is to grasp that Aristotle's ideal form of tragedy is simply this—one in which the destruction of hero or heroine is caused by some false step taken in blindness.[1]

This false step may be either a crime like Clytemnestra's or a mere miscalculation like Dejanira's. It is distortion to read into this theory the moralist's idea of tragic disaster as necessarily the punishment of sin. Here once more the problem of tragedy becomes one with the whole problem of evil. "Poetic justice"—how hard the craving for it has died! Yet to-day it seems merely grotesque to read the sort of explanations in which Gervinus delighted—how Duncan deserved his fate for being so incautious where he went to stay, Desdemona for her carelessness with her pocket-handkerchiefs. We are left cold by the outcry of Lessing at "the mere thought, in itself so terrible, that there should be human beings who can be wretched without any fault of their own". Did this man, we ask, who lived through the horrors of the Seven Years' War, fondly console himself with the thought that all its agonies were deserved? And

---

[1] The *peripeteia* may, it is worth noting, be caused by the mistaken intentions of some *minor* character, like the messenger in *Œdipus*. But *Œdipus* is rather an exceptional case, and Aristotle in his brief discussion does not exhaust the possibilities. His ideal hero needed in any case to show some human frailty, and not be a Sir Charles Grandison (see xv); and so naturally he preferred the neatness and economy of making this frailty the actual cause of the catastrophe.

what a consolation! "Alas, my husband," cried the wife of Socrates, as he was about to drink the hemlock, "you die innocent." "Would you have me die guilty?" was his reply. Yet even Aristotle himself, as we shall see when we come to deal with Character, felt that the misfortunes of absolutely righteous characters were too shocking for the tragic stage (xiii. 2). Poetic justice is not only a fiction; it is not even poetic. And yet this yearning of the human mind to believe the Universe not utterly amoral and indifferent has moulded the whole history of tragedy. For though it is clear that the Tragic Error need not be moral, it is equally clear that it very often has been. Thus we watch Æschylus in play after play struggling with this question of life's justice. If the fathers ate sour grapes, are the children's teeth set on edge? Surely we cannot deny it, when we look on the sinister destinies of generation after generation of Tantalid and Labdacid. And yet, if so, where is justice? Æschylus seems at times to answer with a compromise. Yes, the children's teeth are set on edge; but they do not perish unless they have plucked poison of their own. Crime brings punishment—if not in one generation, then in another. Guilt haunts some families like an evil spirit lurking at the door; but the evil spirit is powerless until the individual takes a first false step. It is like a hereditary predisposition to some disease. The Tragic Error in Æschylus is sometimes, then, that first false step: it is definitely sin, as in the most Hebraic of the Hellenes we should expect it to be. Thus Eteocles commits *hubris*; Agamemnon sacrifices his daughter Iphigeneia to his ambition. Yet even in Æschylus Cassandra goes innocent to slaughter; and Orestes suffers agonies for obeying the word of Apollo.[1]

In Sophocles the tone is widely different. Concerned not to justify life's ways but to show them, he finds no difficulty in representing even the downfall of man doomed before his birth, in the very moment he was begotten. Œdipus has a pride, a hot temper, an imperiousness, that serve to make us dread his fall; but they do not cause it. Dejanira's ruin comes only from her too great trustfulness; Antigone's from her unflinching sense of duty. Still less in Euripides is there any justifying of the ways of God; often they are openly denounced, and the Tragic Error is sometimes not moral, sometimes absent altogether. Iphigeneia and Polyxena are helpless and innocent victims. Hippolytus has sinned only in being righteous overmuch. In short, Euripides was not afraid to break, before it was made, Aristotle's prohibition of the sufferings of innocence. Turn to Shakespeare. Hamlet's Tragic Error is his failure to act; and this is doubtless a moral flaw, such as it is usual to suppose that the *hamartia* must always be. But we must not imagine that, as with Æschylus, this is connected with any sense of a general justice in the world, or that Hamlet's fault merited the frightful punishment it entailed. Hamlet fails to act

[1] For a more Calvinistic view of the inscrutability of man's lot in Aeschylus see the very interesting introduction to the edition of *Agamemnon* by J. D. Denniston and D. L. Page (1957).

and disaster follows: but if we are inclined to suppose that this was a just retribution, we need only turn to the play immediately preceding, where Hamlet's not less noble counterpart does act, only to die despairing on Philippi field. The folly of Lear, the credulity of Othello, the pride of Coriolanus, the love of Antony, or the miscalculation of Romeo—more and more as we examine such examples it becomes clear that their tragic errors serve to make their fate not just, but logical and convincing. In vain Racine with conscious effort tries to make the punishment fit the crime, at least in his prefaces. And if we seek the *hamartia* in more modern tragedy like Ibsen's, it becomes clearer than ever that an intellectual mistake is all that the term need mean. In that clear, bleak, Scandinavian world the root of evil has become more than ever an intellectual thing. Not "be good, sweet maid, and let who will, be clever"—it is the failure to think out situations fundamentally, the weakness of relying on formulæ however noble, that brings to the precipice Brand and Mrs Alving, Nora and Rosmer and the Dead who awake too late. But in general there is one passion above the rest which produces so exactly the blind and pardonable error Aristotle demands, that it is strange to find how little part it plays in that Greek drama on which Aristotle drew. There are only one or two supreme exceptions like *Hippolytus* and *Medea*. The moderns, however, have made up with a vengeance for that ancient neglect, and nine out of ten of our plays have no other spring than Love; so that its blind god seems to have replaced

Dionysus himself as the deity both of our tragic and comic stages, and of their rival, the novel, as well. In vain we weary of his eternal rule; in vain we cry out for other motives than "all the little emptiness of love"; for here is the one fundamental thing which happens to almost all of us, and kindles life for a moment even in the dullest of the living dead. As the frog to the student of biology, so the lover to the anatomist of the human heart; no other creature is at once so universally abundant and so illuminating to handle. No other passion provides so wide an interest and so poignant an appeal. It is well that literature should turn to harp on other heart-strings when it can; but it is well also to recognize that, for our world, love remains the great source of real tragedy. In a peaceful civilization it must be so; in wilder ages, when life itself is in perpetual danger, men may feel more strongly about other things. "Love," says a shrewd fragment of Euripides, "does not vex the man that begs his bread"; and Napoleon, condemning in Racine, as contrasted with Corneille, "une perpetuelle fadeur, un éternel amour", echoes the same truth: "L'amour alors, et plus tard encore, était toute l'affaire de la vie de chacun. C'est toujours le lot des sociétés oisives." But we cannot choose our ages; we might not prefer retreats from Moscow, if we could; in any case women have largely made the civilized society of modern Europe, and it has made love to them in return. Some may feel, in the dry words of Bacon, that "the stage is more beholding to Love than the life of man. For as to the stage, love is ever matter of comedies, and now and then of tragedies. But in life it doth much mischief; sometimes like a syren, sometimes like a fury." But in tragic literature at all events we must recognize the prophetic truth of the cry of Sophocles to "Eros the unconquerable". Love's triumph has indeed fashioned some of the deepest tragedies.

> The asp of Egypt, the Numidian wine,[1]
> My Sigurd's sword, my Brynhild's fiery bed;
> The toll of years of Gudrun's drearihead,
> And Tristram's glaive, and Iseult's shriek are here;
> And cloister-gown of joyless Guinivere.

Such, then, is the essence of Aristotle's theory of the tragic plot. At its best, tragedy is a story of human blindness leading human effort to checkmate itself—a Tragedy of Error. The *hamartia* is the Tragic Error; the *peripeteia*, its fatal working to a result the opposite of that intended; the *anagnorisis*, the recognition of the truth. The error may or may not be moral. And its dramatic importance is not based on any conception of life's justice, but on the purely artistic and logical consideration that it is neater, formally, that calamities should begin at home. After all, the question is not whether the *hamartia* must be wilful sin, but whether sin is ever wilful. The Universe may proceed by law; but, to many, it seems heedless of justice. For its laws are those of cause and effect, not of right and wrong. Similarly in the theatre there may or may not be justice: but there

[1] (Of Sophonisba.)

must be law, not figs growing on thistles, if we are to feel that inevitability which a play needs in order to convince. And the peculiar virtue of the Tragedy of Error is that it is convincing in its logic, neat in its form, poignant in its irony. It remains not the only kind of tragedy; but, as Aristotle says, the best.

VI

CHARACTER

"My stress lay on the incidents in the development of a
soul : little else is worth study."

BROWNING.

OF the characters of tragedy Aristotle stipulates (xv.
1-5) that they must be "good" (but not perfect);
"appropriate" or "true to type"; and "consistent" or
true to themselves.[1] The first of these strikes us at
once as an extraordinary demand. Attempts have
been made by subsequent critics to rationalize it.
"Good", for Corneille (who was always concerned to
make the *Poetics* square as far as possible in retro-
spect with his own past practice), meant "magnificent". Thus his Cléopâtre was wicked, he observed,
but she had greatness of soul. For Dacier and Meta-
stasio, on the other hand, "good" meant "well
marked". But, wriggle as the critics may, it is clear,

---

[1] The tragic character must also be, he says, ὅμοιος—the sense
of which is uncertain: some have rendered it "true to tradition"
(the characters of Greek tragedy being as a rule familiar legendary
figures). That is to say, in Greek tragedy Medea must not be made
too soft-hearted (cf. Horace, *Ars Poetica*, 120-4), just as in a Bible
play Jeremiah could not be represented as a buoyant optimist, or
Herod with a passion for children. But, from other passages in the
Poetics, it seems more likely to mean "like ourselves" in their
general humanity, "natural" (though, of course, on the more heroic
scale of tragic dignity).

if only from the context that "good" (χρηστά) here means "noble", "fine". "Even a woman," continues the ungallant philosopher, "*may* be good; or a slave." And if it seems preposterous that Aristotle should not have risen above such ultra-masculine prejudice, it is only necessary to turn to his *History of Animals* (ix. i. 608B): "Accordingly woman is more sympathetic and easily moved to tears than man, but also more envious and querulous, readier with abuse and blows; and, again, the female sex is more despondent and apprehensive, more shameless, more mendacious, and more deceitful." And as for the scarcity of admirable character in the slave we may remember the words of Homer (though he created Eumaeus the swineherd): "God takes half the worth from a man on the day when slavery comes upon him." For the Greek view is here the exact reverse of Christianity with its praise of the poor and down-trodden; of Christian theory at least.

The real point is, however, that Aristotle is clearly insisting that the *dramatis personæ* of tragedy shall be as *fine* in character as the plot permits. So in Greek sculpture, though a Silenus or a Centaur could not be made to look like an Apollo, they are given so far as possible an idealized beauty of their own. And tragedy in Aristotle's theory represented men as finer than they are, as Polygnotus painted them finer, or as Raphael ennobled the mean presence of St Paul.

To-day we no longer believe in Aristotle's dictum: already Euripides had transgressed it in his pursuit of realism. The poet who was not afraid to bring on the stage characters in rags, was not afraid to bring upon it also ragged souls—mean figures like Jason and that Menelaus in *Orestes* of whom Aristotle complains as unnecessarily vile. (He seems somewhat to forget his own principle that art can make a fine picture even of a toad—as with Iago.) But though we cannot accept this insistence that characters must be as good as possible, in fairness to Aristotle we must remember that with "good" in the Greek sense of the word the principle is not so absurd as it seems to us who have Christian ethics in the background of our minds. To demand that *dramatis personæ* should as far as possible obey the Sermon on the Mount would be far more ridiculous. For the meek do not inherit the world of the theatre. Theirs is the least dramatic of human qualities; and it is seldom that a tragic hero turns the other cheek. But in the different pagan idea of virtue, demanding strength and intensity of character rather than purity of soul, Aristotle's words are not without their force. Greek ethics had a larger element of aesthetics. Machiavelli who found *virtù* even in Cæsar Borgia, has himself vividly expressed the opposition of the two ideals— "Christianity places the supreme good in humility, meekness, and the contempt of worldly things, while Paganism sees it in greatness of soul, strength of body, and all the qualities that make a man formidable." Accordingly, he says, Christianity trains men "to endure evils, not to perform great actions". Indeed it is curious to notice how, under the influence of Machiavelli and Seneca, the characters of many Elizabethan plays are so far from being "good", that the hero and the villain become one and the same; in fact, Marlowe and Marston, Webster and Chapman, provide strange anticipations of the superman "beyond good and evil".

> Give me a spirit that on life's rough sea
> Loves to have his sails fill'd with a lusty wind,
> Even till his sail-yards tremble, his masts crack,
> And his rapt ship runs on her side so low
> That she drinks water and her keel ploughs air.
> There is no danger to a man that knows
> What Life and Death is: there's not any law
> Exceeds his knowledge: neither is it lawful
> That he should stoop to any other law.

But this was a transient phase. Such dragons of the past are all but extinct upon the modern stage, except in melodrama. We have learnt with Meredith

> In tragic life, God wot,
> No villain need be.

It is less often wickedness than weakness that breaks the hearts of modern tragedy. And if Aristotle's rule, that characters must be as fine as possible in the circumstances of the plot, still seems to us rather a naïve and narrow one, as we remember Euripides and Shakespeare and Ibsen, yet among the depressing creatures who populate much modern fiction, with its fear that anything heroic may seem mock-heroic, its preference for mediocre minds and the fall of sparrows rather than of eagles, we may feel that

Aristotle was here not wholly wrong. But we may feel, too, that there is really no rule about the character of tragic characters except that they must have character; and we can only add that not wickedness, but weakness, remains the hardest of all human qualities to make dramatic.

But though Aristotle demanded that the characters of tragedy shall be good, he has also demanded elsewhere (xiii. 2), as we have seen in discussing plot, that the character of the tragic hero shall not be *too* good.

This he arrives at by a rather naïve process of elimination. For, he argues, there is nothing to move pity or fear, or to satisfy men of good will, in seeing a bad character pass from bad fortune to good (as in Maupassant's *Bel Ami*); there is no pity or fear in the passage of a very bad character to a bad end (as with the Jew of Malta or Richard III). On the other hand, the ruin of a man eminently good and just is repugnant and horrible. (Aristotle ignores the case of a good character passing through tribulations to happiness, like Homer's Odysseus, Orestes in *The Eumenides*, Iphigeneia in Tauris, Hermione in *The Winter's Tale*, or Rodrigue and Chimène in *Le Cid*.) So he is left with a hero, not specially outstanding in goodness, nor yet guilty of depravity and wickedness, but only of a tragic error.

This formula seems to me too narrow, the gate too strait. It would exclude on the one hand, if taken literally, leading figures as fine as Prometheus, Antigone, or Hippolytus, Brutus, the Duchess of

Malfi, or Brand; on the other, heroes or heroines as maleficent as Richard III, Vittoria Corombona, or Hedda Gabler.

Aristotle seems to me a little unimaginative in his estimate of the sympathy and pity men can feel for characters very far from being moral paragons. "Compassion," he says (xiii. 2), "is felt for undeserved misfortune." "Tragic pity," echoes one of his latest commentators, "can be felt only for the good." But how prim! I much prefer the poet who hoped, however desperately, that "not a worm is cloven in vain". Macbeth outrages loyalty and hospitality alike, by the cold-blooded murder, under his own roof, of an old man, his king. Webster's Vittoria is a "White Devil". Then there is the Devil himself in *Paradise Lost*, or in Vigny's *Éloa*. Provided a person has *some* redeeming quality— courage, intellect, beauty, wit, passionate devotion; provided they show *some* sort of magnificence—then it is astonishing how much their fellow-men can sometimes forgive them. Just as in real life figures like Mary o' Scots, or Napoleon, or Byron were adored. We do "pity" Vittoria, undaunted before her assassins; or Lady Macbeth, broken and alone with the horror of her guilt; or Macbeth drawing his sword in the face of sure defeat under the walls of Dunsinane. Pity is not so narrow.[1] "The pity of it,

[1] Cf. the story that Racine wrote *Phèdre* to uphold an assertion he had made at Mme. de Lafayette's that a good poet could inspire sympathy even with evil characters, and condonation even for the greatest crimes.

Iago!"—even for Iago at the end. After all, did he
make himself? Hate should be kept for things, not
persons. "They know not what they do."

Still one may agree with Aristotle's principle that
heroes and heroines should not, as a rule, be too
perfect; though not, perhaps with his reason for it.
The objection to perfect characters is not that their
misfortunes are unbearable; it is rather that they tend
to be unbearable themselves. Angels make poor
dramatis personæ. It is human beings that we need.[1]
In the words of the queen of the blameless Arthur—

> He is all fault who has no fault at all,
> For who loves me, must have some touch of earth;
> The low sun makes the colour.

On the other hand the world of to-day has not
much use for Aristotle's demand that characters must
be "appropriate" or "true to type"; indeed a modern
dramatist would be very moderately flattered by
being told that his characters were typical. In the
earlier stages of literature men found it a fascinating
amusement to classify humanity into its various
species; but the classification, once made, quickly
becomes trite, and proves superficial; and so the

[1] That the real reason was artistic, not moral, was already clear
to Boileau (*Art Poétique*, iii):

> Des héros de roman fuyez les petitesses:
> Toutefois aux grands cœurs donnez quelques foiblesses.
> Achille déplairoit, moins bouillant et moins prompt:
> J'aime à lui voir verser des pleurs pour un affront.
> A ces petits défauts marqués dans sa peinture,
> L'esprit avec plaisir reconnoît la nature.

creative artist of the next age studies to avoid the typical as eagerly as his predecessors had sought it. He finds variety by closer observation of the real world in its minuter features—after Æschylus, Euripides; after Corneille, Racine. We can still enjoy the *Characters* of Theophrastus or of Earle; but in so far as such types can find a place on the stage at all, it is less in Tragedy than in the Comedy of Manners. There is no Tragedy of Manners: and we can scarcely believe our eyes as we read Rymer's complaint that Iago is a badly drawn character because soldiers are notoriously an honest class of men. Coleridge indeed writes: "I adopt with full faith the principle of Aristotle, that poetry, as poetry, is essentially ideal, that it avoids and excludes all accident; that its apparent individualities of rank, character, or occupation must be representative of a class; and that the persons of poetry must be clothed with generic attributes, with the common attributes of the class."[1] But many of us may feel more sympathy for the curt summary of Blake's *Notes on Reynolds*: "To generalize is to be an idiot. To particularize is the great distinction of merit." And similarly Yeats in *Plays and Controversies*[2]: "All art is founded upon personal vision, and the greater the art, the more surprising the vision; and all bad art is founded upon impersonal types and images, accepted by average men and women out of imaginative poverty and timidity, or the exhaustion that comes from labour. . . . Our opportunity in Ireland is not

[1] *Biographia Literaria*, xvii.   [2] (1923) pp. 154, 143.

that our playwrights have more talent—it is possible that they have less than the workers in an old tradition—but that the necessity of putting a life that has not hitherto been dramatized into their plays, excludes all these types which have had their origin in a different social order." We can only demand that characters shall not be so eccentric as to prevent us believing in them, or feeling with them. Thus it was at first the stock thing to say that Hedda Gabler was "impossible"; until Grant Allen retorted that he took her down to dinner twice a week. But if we want characters typical enough to seem intelligible, we want them also untypical enough to seem individual.

Modern fiction aided by modern psychology has reached, in writers like Henry James or Proust, subtleties, complexities, and eccentricities undreamed of by Aristotle. He would have been much puzzled by a Swann or a Charlus. And to some extent drama has inevitably shared in this growth of complexity and oddity. Already Hamlet (though the supposed difficulties in understanding him have been mainly invented by critics with too much leisure and too little perception) is a labyrinth beside Clytemnestra or Antigone. Still in psychological elaboration drama cannot keep pace with the novel. The novelist has more space and time; he has more scope for explanatory comment; he can restrict himself to a narrower and subtler public; and what his readers fail to understand at first sight, they can read again.

Aristotle's objection here is simply to figures like

the philosophic Princess Melanippe[1] in Euripides; for it is uncommon for princesses to talk Natural Science. Very likely he would have felt the same of Portia's incursion into a court of law. But we need not dwell on a precept that is partly obvious, partly obsolete; nor yet on Aristotle's other demand for consistency in character, with its saving clause that a person may be consistently inconsistent; as, for instance—

> Varium et mutabile semper
> Femina.

That Virgilian phrase with its insinuation of female fickleness may recall us to dwell for a moment on Aristotle's calm dictum, already quoted, that "even a woman may be a fine character"—so like Pope's sneer, "most women have no character at all". Now it is a curious satire on this supercilious verdict that, though women have never indeed written great tragedy, they have in fact repeatedly dominated it. "In Shakespeare," observes Bernard Shaw, "it is always the woman who takes the initiative." And the extraordinary thing is not only that Shaw's observation proves largely true, but that it is even wider than Shakespeare in its truth and applies, with so few exceptions, to tragedy in general from Æschylus to Ibsen. It remains a strange and almost inexplicable

[1] Melanippe, daughter of Æolus, having borne twin sons to Poseidon, hid them in the cow-house. Her father, thinking it some horrid prodigy that cows should give birth to babies, ordered the infants to be sacrificed. To save them, the princess launched into a learned argument that such phenomena were biologically possible.

fact that in Athena's city, whose citizens subjected their womenfolk to severe restraints, the stage should yet have produced figures like Clytemnestra and Cassandra, Atossa and Antigone, Phædra and Medea, and all the other heroines who dominate play after play of the "misogynist" Euripides. The influence and inspiration of Homer, whose whole world is far nearer to the North with its Brynhilds and its Valkyries, may count for much. And, of course, there were *hetairai* like Aspasia. But the paradox of this world where in real life a respectable woman could hardly show her face alone in the street, and yet on the stage woman equals or surpasses man, has never been satisfactorily explained. In modern tragedy as a whole the same predominance exists. Had it existed here alone, we might have accounted for it on the theory that as plays have been written by men mainly for men, the romantic instinct did the rest. Only in classic Athens, of course, woman was seldom an object of romance. At all events a very cursory survey of Shakespeare's work (similarly with Webster, though not with Marlowe or Jonson) suffices to reveal how this dominance, this initiative of women persists from Rosalind to Lady Macbeth. So too in Racine; six of his tragedies bear their heroines' names; and what male characters of his shall we set against Hermione and Andromaque, Bérénice and Roxane, Phèdre and Athalie? So again with Ibsen; what men shall we match with Solveig and Nora, Hedda and Hilda Wangel and Rebecca West? Even that ruthless realist leaves his women with a touch of the heroic and the ideal. It is an odd, not perhaps a very important fact, but a sufficient answer, I think, to the curious dictum of Aristotle —"even a woman *may* be fine".

Of his last main principle, that characters of either sex should be distinguished persons of high estate, we so little feel the need to-day that it is hard to realize how long it kept its force. At first tragedy was written about the great of the earth simply because, from its religious origins, its characters were of divine or heroic race. And if this custom had arisen by accident, yet there was reason also for its continuance; for Greek tragedy was idealistic, its figures larger than life. Besides, the higher the estate, the greater the fall that follows. As William Painter has written in that prose version of the story of the Duchess of Malfi which Webster used: "So lykewys the fall of a heigh and lofty Tree maketh greater noyse than that which is low and little. Hygh Towers and stately Palaces of Prynces bee seene farther off than the poore Cabans and homely shepheardes sheepecotes: the Walles of lofty Cittyes more a loofe doe Salute the Viewers of the same, than the simple Caves, which the Poore doe digge belowe the Mountayne Rockes." It is first in Euripides that this convention begins to be undermined; here the slave is ennobled, like the woman and the barbarian, while the heroes of legend and the kings of ancient Hellas are brought down to the meaner scale of real life. But the rule died hard. Elizabethan drama might introduce its clowns and its citizens, but its kings and lords remained; and its tragedies of domestic life like *Arden of Feversham*, the obscure ancestors of our modern serious drama, form but a small minority. The French stage as usual was more rigid even than the Greek: where Euripides introduces a simple herdsman in *Iphigeneia in Tauris*, his French imitators would content themselves with nothing meaner than a prince of the blood royal of the Crimea; and the charming young Ion who sweeps the temple steps of Delphi with his broom would have provoked smiles of pity at the Hôtel de Bourgogne. The meanest confidant allowed in their theatre must be a person of the most respectable connections.[1] To-day all is changed. The aristocracy, what is left of it, may still enthral the popular press; but the modern theatre-goer wishes as a rule to see people like himself, characters who are not screened by any divinity of rank from that close scrutiny of the tiniest motives and emotions for which we have come above all to care. Men as they are, not nobler than they are—truth, not splendour—the reactions of the human heart to love and personal relations rather than to crownings and dethronements—these are the subjects of our age. Perhaps we have lost something in what D'Annunzio called "this grey flood of democratic mud," this world of the Welfare State, this stage whose god is sex; though the change seems so inevitable that we can hardly imagine any alternative.

[1] Cf. Fontenelle: "Il faut qu'Ariane soit princesse, tant nous somnes destinés à être toujours éblouis par les titres."

Yet one may wonder if fiction and drama have not swung too far towards the opposite extreme in exchanging the heroic heroes and heroines of the past for the long series of brutes and baggages, toads and trollops, who defile across the pages, or stages, or cinema-screens of to-day. Even when their characters are less degenerate, they remain often depressingly commonplace. "If all we did," wrote T. E. Lawrence (of novel-writing), "was to invent people who were passably real, it would be easier and more realistic yet to go and procreate real children on any woman." This, indeed, seems a little extreme—it was thrown off in a letter. But I share his feeling that creative literature should give its characters both "something keener seen than the earth of our eyes, to set them in" and "something for them to say, better and richer and riper than the stuff we can say ourselves"·

Finally, a word may be said on the somewhat academic issue raised by Aristotle's view that plot is more important than character. "Plot," he says (vi. 14), "is the fundamental thing, the soul of tragedy; whereas character is secondary." This judgment he justifies by an argument not quite worthy of a philosopher. A play, he urges, can be produced without any character-drawing to speak of, but it cannot be produced without a plot; therefore plot is the main thing ($\mu\epsilon\gamma\iota\sigma\tau o\nu$). But surely this confuses the issue. Because a minimum of A may be more indispensable than a minimum of B it does not follow that a maximum of A is more valuable than a maximum of B. We cannot live without a skeleton, but we can live without any higher intellectual life; yet the most superfine skeleton is a minor blessing compared with the infinite possibilities of intellect and character. Nor is there any real force in Aristotle's other argument (even supposing it true) that novices gain skill in character-drawing sooner than in the construction of plots: what of it? The truth is, surely, that the relative importance of character and plot varies with different dramatists and different national temperaments. To the Greek mind or the French, with their sense of how much more a beautiful whole is than the sum of its parts, Aristotle's view may seem true, and *Œdipus* or *Athalie* decisive examples of its truth. Whereas the Englishman, remembering how Shakespeare, with his uncertain handling—sometimes masterly, sometimes childish—of stories in themselves often quite third-rate, has yet created Falstaff and Hamlet, tends to subscribe rather to the opposite dictum of Vanbrugh: "I believe I could show that the chief entertainment as well as the moral lies much more in the Character and the Diction than in the Business and the Event." Certainly in the evolution of Tragedy there has been far more room for the growth of character-drawing than of plot. After Sophocles we may have, from Euripides onward, more complicated, more ingenious, more surprising plots, but hardly more perfect ones; whereas that knowledge of the human heart which is half a science, has progressed like a science, and accumulated subtlety on subtlety. The human mind cannot hover for ever, with Æschylus, like an eagle high above the mountain peaks. It must change; it cannot soar higher; so it descends nearer to the earth and begins to discover the flowers, or weeds, upon the precipices, the whole world of smaller things. What seemed trivial becomes significant. Bacilli turn out to be more dangerous than dragons. The look in a woman's eyes grows more interesting than the rise of dynasties, the dropping of a handkerchief than the falling of the topless towers of Ilium. The climax of a Henry James novel, it has been complained, can consist in one character offering another character a cigarette. With Euripides the Chorus, the representative of the old universality, is already decaying; and in his Medea, we hear instead for the first time the debate of the two contending spirits within a single divided soul. The mighty wind and the earthquake give place to the still, small, dissonant voices heard by him who listens to his own heart. Since then that process has gone on and on. No doubt, as already argued, the most appropriate field for such psychology is not the stage, but the novel. Still this complexity of character, if not the most important thing in modern drama, is the most important sphere of its advance. It was the view of Victor Hugo that, whereas most of the men in an audience wanted action, and most of the women wanted emotion, its thinkers cared above all for character.

There the question must rest; it is confused by the ambiguous overlapping of the two things compared. As Dryden has said: "Every alteration or crossing of a design, every new-sprung passion or turn of it, is a part of the action, and much the noblest, except we conceive nothing to be action till they come to blows." Character and plot grow harder and harder to separate, as the plot takes place more and more inside the character, and the crises of the drama withdraw into the theatre of the soul. Hamlet is the first modern man.

> Action is transitory—a step, a blow,
> The motion of a muscle—this way or that—
> 'Tis done, and in the after vacancy
> We wonder at ourselves like men betrayed:
> Suffering is permanent, obscure, and dark,
> And shares the nature of infinity.

One may, however, wonder how a philosopher who thought the highest life was that of contemplative mental activity could so prefer action to character in this somewhat behaviourist view of drama. Is it not true, rather, that nothing really matters in life but states of mind?

I can only suggest that Aristotle was perhaps something of an extravert. Constantly he stresses activity. Happiness, for him, is the by-product of a personality functioning rightly. He neglects the personal lyric with its expression of mere emotion. Even among metaphors he prefers the active.[1] Character he sees as the product of habitual *action*— as a man becomes a builder by building. "Therefore to be habituated in this way or that, from first youth, makes no small difference. It makes a very great

[1] *Rhetoric*, III. 11. 1.

difference—rather it makes the whole difference"
(*Ethics*, II. 1. 8).

This seems a little over-simple—the education-
alist's usual overestimate of the power of education,
of nurture against nature. Considering the widely
different natures emerging from similar nurture in
figures like Charles II and James II, or indeed in
one's own children, one may grow dubious.

Again, Aristotle was logical, and teleological. The
dispositions and ideas of the characters are only
means to the end of the play, the dénouement of the
plot. Means must be subordinate to ends. If readers
can be divided into epicures, whose taste is above all
for exquisite passages; emotionalists, who want
intoxication; moralists, who stress mental health and
influence-value; and structuralists, who stress form,
organization, integration; then Aristotle, I think,
belongs not only to the third class, but also, very
markedly, to the last.

But in stressing the actions on the stage it may be
that Aristotle forgot a little the reactions of audiences
—how they spontaneously build up an organized
impression (a *Gestalt*) of a personality, as of a face,
from individual features; and how gripping this can
become. (Perhaps that was less important with the
changeless, impersonal, impenetrable masks of the
Attic stage.) Again and again, it seems to me, play
or novel can fail because its public vainly asks—
"Where is the character—or characters—towards
whom I am to feel interest, intimacy, sympathy?"—
that sympathy which remains one of the most vital

things in literature. How dull, too, is history or biography if the author lacks the gift of portraying personality!

In contrast, consider Falstaff—in his own person a vast excrescence on the unity of the Histories, defying the laws of Aristotle as roguishly as those of England. His fascination lies, for me, far less in what he does than in what he is; far less in his rather futile actions—trying to rob carriers, or fooling on Shrewsbury field, or being pinched by fairies—than in his incarnation of "perpetual gaiety", jesting at The Boar's Head or over his oafish recruits. What do I best remember from the scene of his final rejection by the priggish Henry? That one curt, sad comment —because it is so *characteristic*—"Master *Shallow*, I owe you a thousand pound."[1]

Aristotle's opposite attitude may grow clearer if we remember his admiration for *Œdipus the King*. How, ask puzzled readers, could Aristotle say (vi. 11) that a play cannot be written without a plot—a concatenation of actions—but *can* be written without characterization? But in Œdipus we have a man doomed before birth, no matter what his character,

---

[1] Or, to take an example from history, consider the utterance of Napoleon's mother after his death at Saint Helena: "My son died miserably; my other children are proscribed. My grandchildren who promised best, seem doomed to disappear. I am old, forsaken, without glory, without honour—and I would not change places with the first queen in the world." The actions of Madame Mère have little importance; but this reaction, this momentary blaze of character, is like a lightning-flash in the twilight of history. (Cf. Corneille's *Médée*—"What is left you?"—"Myself!")

to parricide and incest. Here, evidently, character is *not* destiny. The plot could be written round a dozen different Œdipuses. (Corneille, for instance, made his Œdipe more stoical.) No doubt Sophocles gives his hero certain personal traits—a touch of arrogance, a hot temper: but these serve to make the audience dread disaster—they do not cause it. The triumph of the piece lies in the skill with which this unhappy type of human impotence in the hands of destiny is made, by fleeing his doom, to run straight into it; by trying to purge his city of the crime, to convict himself of it. In detective-plays character tends to be subordinate to intrigue: and this is the first and most famous of detective-plays.

But *Œdipus* remains, I think, rather exceptional among great plays.[1] Contrast, for example, *Prometheus Bound* or *Samson Agonistes*, where so little occurs before the final catastrophe but conversation and poetry, as visitor after visitor arrives to cast light, each from a different angle, on the solitary hero's character.

Could Aristotle have returned to earth and considered how *The Vicar of Wakefield* succeeds by its characters despite a grotesque plot, and *Tristram Shandy* by its characters almost without a plot at all; how Dickens, despite plots often sentimental or melo-

[1] It is amusing that Fontenelle chooses this same play as example of an unsatisfactory plot. The helpless Œdipus, predoomed by destiny, is, he says, too like a man struck by lightning—"on ne remporte d'Œdipe, et des pièces qui lui ressemblent, qu'une désagréable et inutile conviction des misères de la condition humaine." (*Réflexions sur la Poétique*, xlix). This seems extreme.

dramatic, yet lives by his Gamps and Micawbers; how Flaubert's *Salammbô*, despite desperate labour, a magnificent style, a plot of tragic violence, yet remains a tragic failure largely because we do not care about its persons, especially its heroine—"on ne peut pas la fréquenter"; how *Coriolanus* with a fine plot is yet eclipsed by the more vivid characters of *Antony and Cleopatra*; and with how little plot *The Cherry Orchard* yet holds us in its shadows—then, I think, even Aristotle might have changed his mind. "O brave new world that has such *people* in't"—of how much great work is the secret given by Miranda's cry! And it is just because the people of Miranda's own play seem (except Caliban) rather shadowy beside those of Shakespeare's great period, that *The Tempest* remains for me in comparison, despite neat plot and magic words, "such stuffe As dreames are made on".[1]

Indeed one of the deficiencies of the modern world may seem a certain rarity of vividly individual characters—such as Clemenceau or Churchill. And a pessimist might vision a coming age of Welfare States that would resemble, like some modern histories, the battle-pictures said to have been once painted by a French captive for a Bey of Algiers; where (since Islam forbids representation of living things) there was nothing visible but much smoke, many machines, perhaps some smudgy masses—and not one human individual.

---

[1] Similarly the dénouement of *Cymbeline* is most elaborately and ingeniously plotted; but it does not seem to me the real Shakespeare.

After all, plots are limited. They may not have been wholly exhausted by the ingenious critic who, it is said, wrote a work on "The Thirty-six Dramatic Situations". But they seem to offer a good deal less variety than is to be found in human character. The plots of Scribe and Sardou can be marvels of dexterity; yet their dramas are dead. For they lacked real characters; they lacked ideas and ideals.

I would add that in all plays and novels (though neither Aristotle nor any other critic that I remember has put it so) there is one character that matters more than most of the other figures, often more than all, and sometimes more than the plot—the character of the author himself. His face may be hidden— glimpsed only dimly, as through bars, between the lines. But if that is fine enough, it need not matter even though his personages be poor creatures, or his theme and scene apparently parochial; as, for example, in *Hedda Gabler* or *Madame Bovary*. For there in the background, transfiguring all, shines the indomitable integrity of Ibsen and Flaubert. Aristotle may justly claim (xxiv. 7) that Homer is admirable in speaking through his characters and remaining himself in the background; and Flaubert, that the novelist or dramatist, like God, should be everywhere present in his work, yet nowhere visible. But a fine author, though unseen, is still to be felt.

Spirit with spirit can meet—
Closer is He than breathing, and nearer than hands and feet.

VII

DICTION AND SPECTACLE

THREE of Aristotle's six elements in Tragedy have now been considered—its lyricism, its plot, its character. There remain three more—ideas, diction, and scenic effect. Of the intellectual side of Tragedy, the ideas that the speakers express in language, not much need be said: it is one of the parts of drama which, like its character-drawing, has tended to increase, just as its more lyrical and poetical side has dwindled away. So that in the Discussion Play a species of drama has even been invented in which this element becomes supreme. We can watch the same progress recurring over and over again, from the mysticism of Æschylus to the logic-chopping of Euripides; from the ruthless will of Corneille to the sceptical propaganda of Voltaire; from the thunders of Marlowe to the wit—last breath of a dying drama —of Congreve, Vanbrugh, and Sheridan. The intellect illumines the poet's world like a tropical sun, first quickening, then scorching it to dust and disillusion. "C'est une grande force de ne pas comprendre." But, often as history repeats itself, it does not always do so. And since Ibsen, so intellectual though so much more than merely intellectual, we may perhaps hope that the serious drama has become acclimatized to the harsh light of the critical intelligence and may survive as an oasis in that desert.

As for Diction and Spectacle, the key to the development of these is the perpetual instinct of drama to struggle closer and closer to real life. And, we may add, the closer it has come to life, the nearer it has often been to dying. Tragedy begins as an oratorio: it becomes a conversation overheard in a room, an accident seen in the street. And in its diction and spectacle this effort to become more and more realistic is the ruling tendency.

The terms which a poet uses, said Aristotle (xxi), may be divided into six kinds. First, those current in ordinary speech—that calling a spade "a spade" on which Wordsworth insisted, at least in theory; secondly, foreign terms imported from other languages, or from dialect, like "fey" or "ennui"; thirdly, those which are metaphorical like "cold-blooded"; fourthly, the ornamental periphrasis beloved of eighteenth-century poetry, but now left mainly to the journalist—"the Son of Thetis", "the tame villatic fowl"; fifthly, new coinages like "jabber-wock", or "the fairy *mimbling-mambling* in the garden"; sixthly, forms not entirely invented, but modified by lengthening like "faery", by shortening like "sovran", or by simple variation, as "corse" for "corpse".

Now the poet's style, Aristotle proceeds (xxii), should fulfil, above all, two conditions—"it must be clear and it must not be mean."[1] If it uses only

---

[1] Cf. the indignant contrast drawn by Voltaire between Racine's "Tout dort, et l'armée, et les vents, et Neptune" and Shakespeare's

"current" words, it will be clear but mean, as Wordsworth often is: if it uses only strange words, it will not be mean, but either obscure or jargon, like parts of Sir Thomas Browne or Francis Thompson. Accordingly, "modified" words, variant forms, are useful as being neither mean nor obscure (to-day, however, they are liable to seem affected and conventional). After curtly disposing (xxii. 8) of a certain Aríphrades, who had anticipated Wordsworth's objection to poetic diction, Aristotle then gives his own conclusions. Compounded words, he thinks, are best for the dithyramb (full-dress lyric or ode, which can be richer, because shorter, than epic; like, for instance, *The Hound of Heaven*, or an ode of Keats); rare words suit epic (as we see in Spenser and Milton); whereas metaphorical diction is best suited to the iambic verse of drama. For this is the metre closest to the prose of ordinary life, as befits an imitation of that life; and a poetic diction which is mainly metaphorical can similarly keep closest to the language of ordinary life. "The gift for metaphor," adds Aristotle (xxii. 9), "is the greatest of all. This alone cannot be taught, but is a mark of natural genius; for it implies an inborn eye for likenesses."

To the far-reaching truth of this last statement, disguised as usual in the simple-seeming language of

"Je n'ai pas entendu une souris trotter": and the dismal meanness of some modernizations of the English Bible. On the other hand, clarity is the last thing aimed at by much modern poetry. Perhaps Aristotle fell into the opposite extreme by ignoring that mystery can sometimes have its own impressiveness, and that some language, like some architecture, may gain from a dim religious light.

Aristotle, older criticism hardly, I think, did justice (though the study of imagery has lately become a mania). It was not fully realized how much the art of poetry consists in the somewhat childish pleasure of glimpsing that one thing is like another; in revealing unseen similarities between the unlikeliest objects in the vast, tumbled treasure-chest of the Universe.[1] It is worth taking a speech which bears Shakespeare's stamp on every line, and simply noting how much of its character is due to wealth of metaphor:

> Time hath (my Lord) a wallet at his backe,
> Wherein he puts almes for oblivion;
> A great-siz'd monster of ingratitudes:
> Those scraps are good deedes past,
> Which are devour'd as fast as they are made,
> Forgot as soone as done; perseverance, deere my Lord,
> Keepes honour bright, to have done, is to hang
> Quite out of fashion, like a rustie maile,
> In monumentall mockrie: take the instant way,
> For honour travels in a straight so narrow,
> Where one but goes abreast—keepe then the path:
> For emulation hath a thousand Sonnes,
> That one by one pursue; if you give way,
> Or hedge aside from the direct forthright,
> Like to an entred Tyde, they all rush by,
> And leave you hindmost:
> Or like a gallant Horse falne in first ranke,
> Lye there for pavement to the abject rear,
> Ore-run and trampled on: then what they doe in present
> Though lesse then yours in past, must ore-top yours:
> For time is like a fashionable Hoste,

[1] I have dealt further with this in *Style*, ch. ix.

That slightly shakes his parting Guest by th' hand;
And with his armes out-stretcht, as he would flye,
Graspes in the commer: the welcome ever smiles,
And farewell goes out sighing: O, let not virtue seeke
Remuneration for the thing it was: for beautie, wit,
High birth, vigor of bone, desert in service,
Love, friendship, charity are subjects all
To envious and calumniating time:
One touch of nature makes the whole world kin:
That all with one consent praise new-borne gaudes,
Though they are made and moulded of things past,
And give to dust, that is a little guilt,
More laud then guilt ore-dusted.

Such is that diction of Shakespeare which Dryden described as "pestered with figurative expressions". This gift of metaphor is indeed one of the hardest things to preserve when literatures become literary; and writers like Burns and Synge have succeeded in breathing fresh life into the jaded style of convention simply by going back to the plain vigour of the poor and uneducated, whose minds and vocabulary, instead of dealing in ghostly abstractions, cling still to the concrete. It is worth recalling Synge's preface to *The Play-boy of the Western World*: "Anyone who has lived in real intimacy with the Irish peasantry will know that the wildest sayings in this play are tame indeed, compared with the fancies one may hear in any little hillside cabin in Geesala, or Carraroe, or Dingle Bay. All art is a collaboration. . . . It is probable that when the Elizabethan dramatist took his ink-horn and sat down to his work he used many phrases that he had just heard, as he sat at dinner, from his mother or his children. . . . When I was writing *The Shadow of the Glen*, some years ago, I got more aid than any learning could have given me from a chink in the floor of the old Wicklow house where I was staying, that let me hear what was being said by the servant girls in the kitchen. . . . In a good play every speech should be as fully flavoured as a nut or apple, and such speeches cannot be written by anyone who works among people who have shut their lips on poetry." This hardly needs illustration. A poet like Byron will say, "The tree of knowledge is not that of life"; the Arab tribesman will say, "The tree of silence bears the fruit of peace" in the more sophisticated style of Johnson (himself, however, a master of metaphor) this may turn into the colourless, "Taciturnity is conducive to tranquillity." "Be not thine own worm"—how different is that in force and vividness from "Do not be morbid"! "Thou hast built thy monstrous tower of crime on a foundation of painted smoke," says the Caliph in Flecker's *Hassan*; in the world of Western newspapers that could become, "This supreme crime was devoid of any foundation not completely nebulous." Such *clichés* raise not the ghost of an image. Often the modern writer is like that Orion whose wraith Odysseus saw in Hades, chasing the spectres of the beasts that once in life he slew upon the lonely hills. If we say that we are "well off", not one of us remembers that this is in origin the nautical metaphor of some sailor who had seen the breakers white and threatening on a lee-shore. To-day the phrase is but an empty shell, that has long ceased even to murmur of the sea. "Let us burn our boats," cries the popular orator, "and launch out into the open sea." How are we to breathe any beauty into dramatic speech that imitates a society where men do not even speak, like Monsieur Jourdain, prose?

This denudation of language, this rubbing-down of pointed word and phrase, can be watched in an accelerated form in the diction of the drama from Æschylus to Euripides and Menander, from Marlowe to Shirley and Congreve. It is only in the spendthrift splendour of its youth that Tragedy dares speak gigantically in the "helmeted phrases" of an Æschylus; its prime is as vivid, but less untamed; then come culture and *cliché* and critic. As Goethe put it,

Gute Gesellschaft hab' ich gesehn. Man nennt sie die Gute
Wenn sie zum kleinsten Gedicht keine Gelegenheit giebt.

Epic and lyric may take refuge in the language of other ages, or of none; but the drama dies if it retreats too far from its audience. Where Æschylus had written "mud, the brother of dust"—"war, the money-changer of bodies"—"my hope treads not within the halls of fear"—"the jaw of Salmydessus, step-mother of ships", Euripides made his characters talk often with the bare clearness and matter-of-factness of the law-courts of Athens. From

Was this the face that launched a thousand ships?

or

The multitudinous seas incarnadine,

we pass, at best, to the muted music of the later
Jacobeans on the eve of its final silence, to Ford's

> For he is like to something I remember,
> A great while since, a long, long time ago;

or Shirley's

> Let me look upon my sister now;
> Still she retains her beauty.
> Death has been kind to leave her all this sweetness.
> Thus in a morning have I oft saluted
> My sister in her chamber; sat upon
> Her bed and talked of many a harmless passage.
> But now 'tis night and a long night with her:
> I shall ne'er see these curtains drawn again
> Until we meet in heaven.

So with Racine, the supreme example of the poet
of a sophisticated society, who produces his effects
by a style triumphant in its purity and melody,
though limited to a poverty-stricken vocabulary and
some half-dozen threadbare images that come
marching round and round like a stage-army.

If the theatre shows in accelerated form the
general wearing-down of language into something
more and more abstract, plain, and prosaic, that may
be because the ordinary decline of vivid speech is
reinforced by that tendency toward dramatic realism
which turns from gazing at the heavens to become a
microscope focussed on the tiniest fibres of the
human heart. Hence an inevitable change from gong
and cymbal to the bald, broken speech of daily life.
And as in diction, so in metre; from the rhythmic

pomp of Æschylus we pass to the tripping iambics
of Euripides; from Marlowe's thunderous

> Usumcasane and Theridamas,
> Is it not passing brave to be a king
> And ride in triumph through Persepolis?

to the prosodic shamble of Shirley's

> He had better cool his hot blood in the frozen
> Sea, and rise hence a rock of adamant
> To draw more wonder to the north, than but
> Attempt to wrong her chastity.

And to-day?—is verse-drama dead? Was it already
past cure when Dryden and his fellows tried to
galvanize it with the heroic couplet? In French
literature *Hernani* seems now a gigantic *pastiche*; and
Faust is rather a poem than a play. Even could we
listen to a modern tragedy in blank verse, our poets
have forgotten how to write it for the stage, our
actors how to speak it. Since Dryden, only Beddoes
and Bottomley have, I think, produced first-rate
dramatic verse, and the verse is the only thing
dramatic in the dramas of Beddoes. And if to-day
blank verse will no longer serve us, it is not likely
that any other metre will; for it is hardly possible
for verse to come nearer prose, without becoming
prose. Yet even if good dramatic blank verse could
be written, it would tend to produce the wrong effect
and the wrong atmosphere. It has too much of a
past; too many memories that cast a sort of glamour
of unreality and remoteness over its content. The old

objection to rhyme on our stage, that for the English
ear it at once suggests the atmosphere of a fairy-tale,
has come to apply to blank verse also. There may
perhaps be no real reason why it should not be as
minutely truthful to the psychology of real life as we
now require; but it would not seem so.[1] If blank
verse is good, it seems mock-Elizabethan: and if it
is bad, it is frightful.

Recently there have been attempts to write plays
in a form intermediate between blank verse and
prose. They do not seem to me very successful; not,
at least, for those who feel, like Johnson, that blank
verse, unless splendid, becomes merely crippled

[1] Professor Bonamy Dobrée in his interesting discussion of
dramatic diction, entitled *Histriophone,* objects to modern verse-
playwrights on the ground of their slowness, as contrasted with the
perfect stage-prose of Shakespeare or Congreve. This seems to me
true. We may recall Coleridge's description of Schiller as moving in
his blank-verse "like a fly in a glue-pot"; but I find it all the more
difficult to accept the contradictory suggestion earlier in Professor
Dobrée's essay that in Elizabethan drama prose is used as a *slower*
alternative to verse. In verse the voice pauses not only when sense,
but also when metre, demands—at the ends of lines and on syllables
often unimportant in themselves; how then can it be *more* rapid
than prose, where the proportion of lightly tripping, unstressed
syllables is higher, and the only pauses are those of the sense? When
an Elizabethan passes from verse to prose it is simply as if he came
down off his pedestal, threw aside his singing-robes, stretched his
arms, and relaxed. The relaxation may be simply that of rest, or of
humour after seriousness, or of cynicism and disillusion; as, for
instance, when Hamlet breaks into that famous prose passage
beginning with "majestical roof, fretted with golden fire", but
ending with a shrug of the shoulders—"Man delights not me; no,
nor woman neither, though by your smiling you seem to say so."
Prose has more latitude in its speed, as in other respects; but that it
is generally slower in its effect than verse I cannot believe.

prose. After the opening speeches of a play in this form I found myself murmuring, "Thank God, at least it is not in verse"; only to discover next day, in a bookshop, that it *was*.

But if verse-tragedy has become impossible on the modern stage, and a sickly hot-house plant—with a few fine exceptions like *Atalanta in Calydon* and *The Duke of Gandia*—as a form of literature, there remains the question whether serious drama must give up poetry as well as verse. "Ibsen," wrote Yeats, "has sincerity and logic beyond any writer of our time, and we are all seeking to learn them at his hands; but is he not a good deal less than the greatest of all times, because he lacks beautiful and vivid language?" It is hard to judge the style of an author known to most of us only in translation; but, granted that most modern serious drama, being realistic, has and can have little poetry in its style, it may yet preserve a certain poetry in its ideas. The phrases of Ibsen that we remember are mostly ironical or epigrammatic; but about his situations and his figures, especially in the latest plays, a strange poetry still clings, as it clings about the people of the Icelandic sagas for all the bleak brevity of their prose. It can be like the sudden, unexpected beauty of the factory stacks of some modern town seen under their canopy of smoke against the red of evening. And since we live in an age of factory chimneys, it is better to gain eyes for such new beauty than to try to recreate the old loveliness by painting them green, with imitation branches, to resemble trees.

And, in other ways, too, other modern dramatists have succeeded in keeping a poetry of phrase and rhythm without lapsing into the unreality of verse.

"On ne sait pas.[1] . . . Et qu'est-ce que l'on sait? . . . Elle était peut-être de celles qui ne veulent rien dire, et chacun porte en soi plus d'une raison de ne plus vivre. . . . On ne voit pas dans l'âme comme on voit dans cette chambre. Elles sont toutes ainsi. . . . Elles ne disent que de choses banales; et personne ne se doute de rien. . . . On vit pendant des mois à côté de quelqu'un qui n'est plus de ce monde et dont l'âme ne peut plus s'incliner; on lui répond sans y songer: et vous voyez ce qui arrive. . . . Elles ont l'air de poupées immobiles, et tant d'évènements se passent dans leurs âmes. . . . Elles ne savent pas elles-mêmes ce qu'elles sont. . . . Elle aurait vécu comme vivent les autres. . . . Elle aurait dit jusqu'à sa mort: 'Monsieur, Madame, il pleuvra ce matin'; ou bien 'Nous allons déjeuner, nous serons treize à table'; ou bien 'Les fruits ne sont pas encore mûrs.' Elles

---

[1] Maeterlinck, *Intérieur*. This little play is interesting also as a return to that primitive form of drama where the chorus was everything and action almost absent. For it consists mainly of a dialogue between a stranger and an old man, reflecting on a tragedy that has already taken place. A girl has been drowned, perhaps drowned herself; the body is being brought home from the river, but meanwhile the girl's family are seen in the background sitting in their lighted room, unconscious of what is approaching step by step—mute figures from first to last. For Maeterlinck's theory of a Static Drama, which shall stop and think, like Greek Tragedy, instead of passing from beginning to end in a whirlwind of murders and adulteries, see *Le Trésor des Humbles*.

parlent en souriant des fleurs qui sont tombées et pleurent dans l'obscurité. . . . Un ange même ne verrait pas ce qu'il faut voir; et l'homme ne comprend pas qu'après coup. . . . Hier soir, elle était là, sous la lampe comme ses sœurs et vous ne les verriez pas, telles qu'il faut les voir, si cela n'était pas arrivé. . . . Il me semble les voir pour la première fois. . . . Il faut ajouter quelque chose à la vie ordinaire avant de pouvoir la comprendre. . . . Elles sont à vos côtés, vos yeux ne les quittent pas; et vous ne les apercevez qu'au moment où elles partent pour toujours. . . . Et cependant, l'étrange petite âme qu'elle devait avoir; la pauvre et naïve et inépuisable petite âme qu'elle a eue, mon enfant, si elle a dit ce qu'elle doit avoir dit, si elle a fait ce qu'elle doit avoir fait!"

"Salomé,[1] vous connaissez mes paons blancs, mes beaux paons blancs, qui se promènent dans le jardin entre les myrtes et les grands cyprès. Leurs becs sont dorés, et les grains qu'ils mangent sont dorés aussi, et leurs pieds sont teints de pourpre. La pluie vient quand ils crient, et quand ils se pavanent la lune se montre au ciel. Ils vont deux à deux entre les cyprès et les myrtes noirs et chacun a son esclave pour le soigner. Quelquefois ils volent à travers les arbres, et quelquefois ils couchent sur le gazon et autour de l'étang. Il n'y a pas dans le monde d'oiseaux si

---

[1] Wilde, *Salomé*: influenced by Maeterlinck, from whose plays passages might have been quoted much more similar to this than the speech from *Intérieur*.

merveilleux. Il n'y a aucun roi du monde qui possède
des oiseaux aussi merveilleux. Je suis sûr que même
César ne possède pas d'oiseaux aussi beaux. Eh bien!
Je vous donnerai cinquante de mes paons. Ils vous
suivront partout et au milieu d'eux vous serez comme
la lune dans un grand nuage blanc. . . . Je vous les
donnerai tous. Je n'en ai que cent, et il n'y a aucun
roi du monde qui possède des paons comme les
miens, mais je vous les donnerai tous. Seulement, il
faut me délier de ma parole et ne pas demander ce
que vous m'avez demandé."

"Ah, cara, tutto il vostro sangue e tutte le vostre
lacrime non potrebbero far rivivere un solo sorriso![1]
Tutta la bontà della primavera non potrebbe far
rifiorire una pianta che è lesa alla radice. Non vi
tormentate dunque, Bianca Maria, non vi dolete
delle cose che sono già compiute, che sono già del
tempo. Io ho già messo i miei giorni e i miei sogni
fuori dell'anima mia:—i giorni che sono passati, i
sogni che si sono spenti. Io vorrei che nessuno avesse
pietà di me, che nessuno tentasse di consolarmi.
Vorrei trovare qualche cammino tranquillo per i
miei piedi incerti, qualche luogo dove il sonno e il
dolore si confondessero, dove non fosse strepito nè
curiosità, nè alcuno vedesse o ascoltasse. E vorrei
non più parlare, giacchè in certe ore della vita

---

[1] D'Annunzio, *La Città Morta*. It is not necessary to know
Italian to appreciate at least some of its general style and sound and
effect.

nessuno sa quali parole sia meglio dire e quali sia meglio tenere per sè. E vorrei, vorrei, Bianca Maria, che voi aveste fede in me come in una sorella maggiore, andatasene quietamente per aver tutto compreso e tutto perdonato . . . quietamente . . . quietamente . . . non lontano . . . non troppo lontano."

"Draw[1] a little back with the squabbling of fools when I am broken up with misery. I see the flames of Emain starting upward in the dark night; and because of me there will be weasels and wild cats crying on a lonely wall where there were queens and armies and red gold, the way there will be a story told of a ruined city and a raving king and a woman will be young for ever. I see the trees naked and bare, and the moon shining. Little moon, little moon of Alban, it's lonesome you'll be this night, and to-morrow night, and long nights after, and you pacing the woods beyond Glen Laoi, looking every place for Deirdre and Naisi, the two lovers who slept so sweetly with each other. . . .

"I have put away sorrow like a shoe that is worn out and muddy, for it is I have had a life that will be envied by great companies. It was not by a low birth I made kings uneasy, and they sitting in the halls of Emain. It was not a low thing to be chosen by Conchubor, who was wise, and Naisi had no match for bravery. It is not a small thing to be rid of

[1] J. M. Synge: *Deirdre of the Sorrows.*

grey hairs, and the loosening of the teeth. It was the choice of lives we had in the clear woods, and in the grave, we're safe, surely. . . . .

"I have a little key to unlock the prison of Naisi you'd shut upon his youth for ever. Keep back, Conchubor; for the High King who is your master has put his hands between us. It was sorrows were foretold, but great joys were my share always; yet it is a cold place I must go to be with you, Naisi; and it's cold your arms will be this night that were warm about my neck so often. . . . It's a pitiful thing to be talking out when your ears are shut to me. It's a pitiful thing, Conchubor, you have done this night in Emain; yet a thing will be a joy and triumph to the ends of life and time. (*She presses the knife into her heart.*)"

After that go back and read the blank verse of Tennyson's *Queen Mary* or Browning's *Blot in the Scutcheon*; they seem written in butter. The thing to note about these four passages is the similarity of their solutions of the same problem—how to find a serious dramatic diction free from the dead hand of verse, yet not too close to life for art. They differ in many ways; and many other varying solutions can no doubt be found; but these four have in common a certain simplicity, a patterned repetition of phrases to replace the patterned repetition of metre, and a pronounced rhythm. Verse is a rhythm of one pattern, repeated over and over again; here the rhythm is of many patterns and not regularly repeated; but the verbal repetitions partly compensate. There is a real danger, in this simplified style, of dropping into affectations and *niaiseries*. But whatever the language of the theatre of the future, I do not see that the poets of the nineteenth century have produced any convincing answer to the demand made by Stendhal nearly a century and a half ago that drama must abandon verse.[1] Thrice a great school of tragedy has died with the decay of poetry; let us be thankful that drama has learnt at last to live in prose.

Of the spectacular, the last of the six elements he names in Tragedy, Aristotle has written only a few words, though very much to the point. "Fear and pity," he says, "can be produced by spectacular means; but it is much better to produce them by the way you write your play." He may perhaps have been thinking of things like that famous first performance of *The Eumenides* of Æschylus when the audience, says tradition, was frozen with horror, and women miscarried in the theatre at the terrible appearance of the Erinyes.[2] In any case this is another of those

---

[1] In *Racine et Shakespeare* (1824). It is true that his objection was rather to the French Alexandrine with its conventional vocabulary, "qui dit toujours trop ou trop peu et qui sans cesse recule devant le mot propre", than to our blank verse with its greater freedom. But he definitely demanded prose-tragedy: the answer, though not exactly the answer Stendhal expected, was Ibsen.

[2] The Renaissance, of course, could be far cruder; cf. *Cambises*, with a flaying alive upon the stage; *Titus Andronicus*; and the

platitudes of Aristotle's which human nature has always persisted in ignoring, and so has to relearn by bitter experience over and over again. The drama has suffered from three enemies above all—the puritan, the pedant, and the theatre-manager; and of these the last has sometimes been the worst; for the ideal of those who stage plays has often been to allow nothing whatever to remain imaginary in a performance, except its dramatic merit. They have often been denounced; but they have been able successfully to appeal to the populace. Even in the ages of happiest simplicity in the theatre we may suspect that the means rather than the will was lacking to spoil it; and that the Elizabethans, whose methods seem on the whole so superior to ours, might themselves have welcomed the worst abortions of nineteenth-century realism. The Greek stage was plain, perforce; their conventions were simple owing to their religious origin, and remained so owing to religious conservatism. They even did without that darkening of the stage which seems to us one of the least dispensable aids to the weakness of our imagination. Those tall, padded figures, moving slowly like Easter Island statues in front of their changeless architectural setting, were in little danger of overleaping the barrier between art and realism. A few rags were the limit of the innovations even of Euripides. To what the Greek had thus created, the Roman added

suggestion of the Dutch scholar Vossius for heightening dramatic effects by executing real criminals in tragedies (as was actually done in the mimes of Roman decadence under the Empire).

nothing except what money could buy—vulgarity.
We might be already at Drury Lane.

> The curtain is kept down[1] four hours or more,
> While horse and foot go hurrying o'er the floor,
> While crownless majesty is dragged in chains,
> Chariots succeed to chariots, wains to wains,
> Whole fleets of ships in long procession pass,
> And captive ivory follows captive brass. . . .
> You'd think you heard the Gargan forest roar
> Or Tuscan billows break upon the shore,
> So loud the tumult waxes when they see
> The show, the pomp, the foreign finery.
> Soon as the actor, thus bedizened, stands
> In public view, clap go ten thousand hands.
> "What said he?" Nought. "Then what's the attraction?"
>   Why,
> That woollen mantle with the violet dye.[2]

Eighteen centuries later Pope echoed what history
had repeated.

> The Play stands still; damn action and discourse,
> Back fly the scenes, and enter foot and horse;
> Pageants on pageants, in long order drawn,
> Peers, Heralds, Bishops, Ermin, Gold, and Lawn . . .
> Ah, luckless Poet! stretch thy lungs and roar,
> That Bear or Elephant shall heed thee more;
> While all its throats the Gallery extends,
> And all the Thunder of the Pit ascends!
> Loud as the Wolves on Orcas' stormy steep,
> Howl to the roarings of the Northern deep.

[1] In the Roman theatre curtains were lowered, instead of being raised like ours.

[2] Horace, *Epistles*, II. i. 189 ff: Conington's translation.

Such is the shout, the long-applauding note,
At Quin's high plume, or Oldfield's petticoat.

In a word, the progress of spectacle, as of diction,
in drama may be summed up as an ever-increasing
realism. And it is a commonplace now that in the
English theatre this process can be watched step by
step with particular clearness in the transformation
of the Platform to the Picture Stage, and the gradual
divorce of actors from audience. The audience in the
Greek theatre, without a curtain and with a chorus,
was closely united to the stage which they half sur-
rounded; still more the Elizabethans with their
Apron Stage. It was the Restoration which first
began to push back the actors into the midst of the
newly introduced scenery, and behind the proscen-
ium arch which that scenery involved—the destined
frame of the Picture Stage. The mid eighteenth
century thrust the last spectators off the stage; and
the early nineteenth finally abolished the Apron, thus
cutting at the root of soliloquy and aside. The more
perfect methods of lighting became, the greater grew
the gulf between actor and public[1]; and Edison with
his electric bulb can claim no obscure place in the
annals of the theatre. So it came about that the drama,
like the human race in Samuel Butler's forecast,
became the slave of its own machines. In the
eighteenth century, as in the fourth century B.C., the

[1] The tendency for drama to become merely spectacular was
aggravated by the anomaly that till 1843 only three theatres were
allowed in London; accordingly those three grew ever vaster and
less suited to real acting.

dramatist was overshadowed by the actor; in the nineteenth, as in the Rome of Augustus, the actor in his turn by the carpenter and machinist. Yet wisdom comes often by excess; and from the abuse of mechanism we may learn its use, as common sense, aided by the film, kills the sort of drama which was predominantly spectacle. For those who desire to gape at moonrise over Portia's Belmont, or a realistic shipwreck in *The Tempest*,[1] or to see a railway accident rendered to the life, can gape twice as wide and as cheaply in a village picture-palace. The theatre, despite the original meaning of its name, needs an audience, not spectators; and it is excellent that those whose only sense is visual, should have elsewhere to go. It is indeed not so much better and less vulgar scenery and spectacle that we want, as less scenery and spectacle altogether. Here, I think, lay the danger of such artists as Gordon Craig, with those superb settings which would make us forget that "the play's the thing". Cover the Tragic Muse with gold paint, even the best gold paint, and she stifles. We do not want Stork in exchange for Log. If Blake himself came and offered his services as scene-painter, we might be wise to refuse him as tactfully as possible. Better the Chinese stage with a chair for a canoe, two candlesticks and an image for a temple. Under the tyranny of the star actor we may

---

[1] As produced early in this century at His Majesty's under Beerbohm Tree, this was almost enough to make one seasick. It delighted my childish eyes; but not some of the ladies in the audience.

have the Prince of Denmark without *Hamlet*; under the tyranny of the scenic artist the scenery can kill the drama. We do not want lighting effects that make us catch our breath—or we shall have no breath left to catch over the tragic climax, and fail to see the play for the lighting. Such exaggerations are as bad as the sort of actor who cannot speak a line without flapping about the stage. The drama, indeed, is lost when the eye begins to steal from the ear. No doubt great dramatists have valued visual effects in due season— as Æschylus with the tumultuous crowds of his *Supplicants*, or Racine at the climax of *Athalie*. But dangerous they remain.

This may be seen, I think, in films of Shakespeare. They can be delightful in themselves; they can reveal Shakespeare from new angles, as can performances in modern dress (though these tend to buffoonery, and soon become a bore). None the less Henry V or Richard III is apt to become dwarfed by the landscapes of Agincourt or Bosworth Field; Hamlet, by the towering architecture of Elsinore. Even the archaeological details, fascinating in themselves, can distract. Things begin to dominate people, where people should dominate things.

There are perhaps three main dangers in modern civilization—that men may grow dwarfed in giant cities and states; that men may lose their independence and individuality in a desire to conform, fostered by the cult of the common man, equality, and democracy (not a good form of government, merely the best of a poor lot); and that the personal element in life may be cramped and crushed by the spread of science and mechanization. There are too many machines in the world, too many people, and too few individuals. All these dangers can be seen in filmed classics. What Aristotle said of the scenic element and the spectacular has not lost its force[1].

[1] For an excellent analysis of Ibsen's admirable skill in deepening dramatic effect by subtleties of lighting, staging, and dress, see J. Northam, *Ibsen's Dramatic Method* (1953).

VIII

THE THREE UNITIES AND COMIC RELIEF

Qu'en un lieu, qu'en un jour, un seul fait accompli
Tienne jusqu'à la fin le théâtre rempli.

BOILEAU

THE interest of the Three Unities is mainly historical, but a brief outline of their development may
be added here. It provides among other things a very
clear, and unfavourable, example of the influence of
critics on creative artists. Two main reasons were
adduced in support of this strange trinity, both false
—that Aristotle had enjoined them; and that without
them a play would be, not inferior in artistic form,
but incredible. It was the name, above all, of realism
that was invoked to defend a rule responsible in
practice for some of the most fantastically unreal
situations in drama

Aristotle had in fact insisted only that the action
must have an artistic unity, free of irrelevances. He
had also remarked, without forming any theory about
it, that the duration of plays was in practice generally
limited to twenty-four hours or a little more. The
Unity of Place he never so much as mentions.[1] The

[1] Hence de Tocqueville's wicked wit about the brief liaison of
Mérimée with George Sand is untrue at least as regards Aristotle
—"On assure même qu'ils avaient conduit leur roman suivant les
règles d'Aristote et qu'ils en avaient réduit toute l'action a l'unité
de jour et de lieu."

Greek theatre, with a chorus and without a curtain, did in fact generally observe the Unities of Time and Place. Without a curtain the transition would have been difficult; and with a chorus, it was unlikely that the same dozen old men should reappear, all together now at Athens, now at Sparta, now at Thebes; still more, that they should punctually reassemble at intervals of years. Still the convention of a choric ode covers an interval of some time in *The Persians*, *Agamemnon*, *The Women of Trachis*, *Œdipus at Colonus*, and *The Suppliants* (of Euripides); and there are changes of place in *Ajax* (from the hero's tent to the seashore) and in *The Eumenides* (from Delphi to Athens).[1]

Passing to later times, we find Horace insisting, like Aristotle, on unity of action only. It is at the Renaissance that the mischief begins. Trissino's *Poetica* (1529-49) and Cintio (1554) reasserted the Unity of Time: Robertelli (1548) narrowed it to twelve hours ("no work is done at night"), while others as arbitrarily limited the epic to one year. Scaliger (1561) cut down the allowance still further to from six to eight hours; but the phrase, "les Unités Scaligériennes" is a misnomer; and the real discredit of formulating the "Three Unities" seems to belong to Castelvetro (1570). The idea now spread like the plague, that no intelligent person's imagination could lend credence to a play that was so unreal as to represent more than one place or one day.

---

[1] For the extreme freedom of the lost *Stheneboea* of Euripides, see my *Greek Drama for Everyman*, 11.

Sidney preached it; Jonson praised himself for practising it in *Volpone*, and railed at less correct playwrights in the prologue to *Every Man in his Humour*. But the victory of the critics over the artists was finally won when Richelieu, Chapelain, and the Academy conquered Corneille; who was converted to propound that the supposed duration of a play should equal the time it took to act, and that its action should be circumscribed within a single city. Milton agreed; but Dryden brought respectful objections to the cramping effects of such rules, and they always sat uneasily on English shoulders. Dennis might urge the plea of *vraisemblance* in its crudest form: "A reasonable man may delude himself so far as to fancy that he sits for the space of twelve Hours without removing, eating, or sleeping, but he must be a Devil that can fancy he does it for a Week." But Congreve, in the dedication of *The Double Dealer* (1694), complains with truth that the Unities cost endless pains in the observance without much repayment in the result; and Farquhar in his *Discourse of Comedy* appeals with a persuasive gesture from "Aristotle" to Pit, Box, and Galleries. It only remained, as far as the English stage was concerned, for Johnson to sweep what was left of the Unities into the wastepaper basket, in the Preface to his *Shakespeare*. "He that can take the stage at one time for the palace of the Ptolemies, may take it in half an hour for the promontory of Actium. . . . And where is the absurdity of allowing that space to represent first Athens, and then Sicily, which was always known to be neither Sicily nor Athens, but a modern theatre?" It is true that, as Coleridge was to point out, Johnson exaggerates the consciousness of the spectator's disbelief, whereas it is most of the time only subconscious and suspended; and, in consequence, Johnson's attack is open to the objection that similar arguments could be used against any theatrical illusion—why dress up as a medieval king with crown and sceptre a man who is known to be neither medieval nor a king, but a hireling at ten pounds a week? "Why, indeed?" some may say. But we do need some assistance in suspending our disbelief, and the point is merely that the Unities of Time and Place are superfluous, because their infringement is found in practice to offer no real difficulty to the imagination. It is a winged creature, not a snail. But the passage in Johnson's Preface remains one of the finest and wittiest things in his or any criticism. Little more has since been heard in England of the Three Unities, and Johnson's passage was effectively stolen by Stendhal for his attack on them in France. As an aid to illusion they were never worth what they cost in other ways; how needless they are for illusion, the cinema has further shown; but, as an aid to artistic economy and perfection of form, something may still be gained from a modified respect for them.[1]

In connection with the Unity of Action, to the

[1] From a practical point of view it may be safer, in moderation, to disregard strict Unity of Time than of Place; too much scene-shifting is likelier to lead to loss of money, time, and continuity.

infringement of which it has often led, a word may
be said also of Comic Relief. Here, too, neo-classic
criticism since the Renaissance shows its curious
tendency to out-Greek the Greeks in strictness.
Aristotle indeed says that Tragedy represents an
action which is "serious"; and Greek Tragedy in
practice has little Comic Relief; yet it has some. This
will be found, indeed, like most things of literary
value, already existing in Homer; whose gods are
sometimes used for this purpose, as well as men like
Thersites or Irus. Again, the tragic trilogy was
regularly followed by a tragic burlesque, called a
satyric drama, of which our one complete specimen is
the *Cyclops* of Euripides. Further, the Nurse in *The
Choephoræ*, Oceanus in *Prometheus*, the Messengers
in *Antigone* and *The Bacchæ*, the Phrygian of *Orestes*,
are all partly comic figures; still more the Menelaus
of *Helen* and the rollicking Heracles of *Alcestis*,
which may claim to be the world's first romantic
comedy, and was in fact a substitute for the ordinary
satyric drama. We may recall, too, the famous
passage at the close of Plato's *Symposium*, where
among the empty wine-cups in the grey of dawn
Socrates explains to the sleepy Aristophanes and
Agathon that the same genius should be supreme in
comedy and tragedy alike—the first whisper, as it
were, of the coming of Shakespeare.

For the Middle Ages, which did not know what
"incongruous" meant, and could illuminate even the
margin of a missal (like that which Charles V gave
his mistress) with apes at play, the mixture of tragic

and comic was as natural as breathing, and it produced their best dramatic work. The Townley Shepherds, or the Doctor's Servant in *The Play of the Sacrament*, redeem pages of pious and wooden earnestness. Further, it was this medieval tradition, transmitted through popular interludes like *Cambises* and *Horestes*, that saved the English stage from the unmitigated solemnity of the Classical pedants and the tradition of tragedy according to Seneca. In vain the protests of Sidney and his like at this mixture of "funerals and hornpipes." Nor were choric odes of much use with an Elizabethan audience as a relief to the tension of tragedy; tragedy possessed no horrors which were not a relief after an ode in the style of *Gorboduc*. The greatest Elizabethan tragedy is half the child of comedy, not only because Polonius and Macbeth's Porter and Lear's Fool produce some of its most striking scenes. Character, too, gains as much as plot; and the tragedies do not profit more by the addition of comic scenes than some of the tragic characters by the acquisition of a sense of humour. Sometimes, indeed, Shakespeare's protagonists remain throughout as serious as those of Sophocles: we hear no laughter from Macbeth or Othello. But for that very reason Hamlet and Cleopatra seem to mark a new era in the portrayal of human nature on the tragic stage.

Henceforth English drama hardly needed the arguments of Dryden and Johnson to maintain its tradition of comic relief: but in France the unsmiling severity of the tragic mask remained unrelaxed for another two centuries; and it is still worth reading Hugo's attack on it in the preface to his *Cromwell*.

Even in our own day Mr T. S. Eliot has argued that, though human nature may permanently crave for comic relief, "that does not mean that it is a craving that ought to be gratified. It springs from a lack of the capacity for concentration. . . . The doctrine of *Unity of Sentiment*, in fact, happens to be right." But I do not follow why permanent human cravings should be thus loftily ignored by artists whose function is, surely, in part that they "live to please". And comic relief seems often artistically valuable. Just as the ancient Persians deliberated on weighty decisions, first drunk, then sober, or *vice versa*, so as to see the matter from widely different viewpoints; just as a surveyor likes to get bearings on an object from widely separated positions; so one may gain by seeing characters and actions from the opposite standpoints of grave and gay. The contrast may give new depth. The characters may grow rounder. (And I prefer both men and books that can smile.)

Further, if it is a question of concentration, an audience may concentrate better on crises if it has relaxed at moments in between. Anyone who has watched a chick struggling out of its shell realizes how often Nature's way is—"Strain—rest—strain—rest". There is matter for thought in a comment of Mérimée's. Having planned his *Chambre Bleue* to end tragically, "I naturally began it in a gay tone." Then he changed to a happy ending. "I ought to have rewritten the first part in a tragic tone; but it was too much trouble."

The only conclusion seems tolerance. There is no reason why a tragedy must be as laughterless as the house of Rosmersholm, and equally no reason why it should not. Only one rule remains about humour in Tragedy; that it must not clash with the tone of the whole. It is extraordinary how seldom this fault is found in Shakespeare, and how often in his contemporaries and successors. Mercutio and Thersites, Pandarus and Polonius, the Grave-diggers and the Porter and Cleopatra's Clown seem inconceivable in any play but their own. Nature herself does not colour her creatures more perfectly to their surroundings. It is far otherwise with *The Changeling*, or *Venice Preserved*, or Flecker's *Hassan*.

"Laugh, my young friends," says Nietzsche, "if you are at all determined to remain pessimists." And again, "True, I am forest and a night of dark trees; but he that is not afraid of my darkness will find banks of roses under my cypresses." So in Tragedy; beneath her cypresses we tend to need either that laughter, or the roses of poetry, or both; and the Tragic Muse has learnt that, to hold her hearers, she must either sing sometimes, as in her Greek girlhood, or sometimes smile.

IX

CONCLUSION

TRAGEDY, then, is simply one fruit of the human instinct to tell stories, to reproduce and recast experience. And since experience is often sad, so are its copies. The religious ceremonies out of which Tragedy has twice arisen, chanced to lend themselves to the dramatic impulse, as the cavern-wall lent itself to the caveman's magic paintings of bison and mammoth; and so ritual became art. Last came the philosophers to explain this picture of life, just as they explained life itself; and in both cases their explanations seem often nonsense. To-day as we look back on the past we may wonder how little good tragedy, or indeed good drama of any sort, has resulted from the efforts of so many centuries, as compared, for instance, with the vast amount of good lyric poetry or prose fiction in the world. And yet this is only to be expected, when we consider that drama is much more dependent on a peculiar combination of social circumstances, on the existence of good audiences and good acting, as well as of good dramatists; dependent also on a wide combination of gifts in the writer himself, who has a complicated organ to play on, with many stops, and no simple Arcadian pipe. And what of the future? The prospects, while our society remains as it is, seem

interesting rather than brilliant. Up to a point, with
the growth of complexity in the study of character,
the serious drama has progressed, though it has paid
for that specialization by the loss, first of its musical,
and then largely of its poetical elements. But a time
comes when the analysis of character becomes too
intricate for the stage. You cannot dramatize Proust.
With primitive man, to think is to act; with his rather
more civilized successors, to think is at least to speak;
but to-day the human feelings we dwell on are often
submerged in silence, often in preconsciousness. At
crises men gaze into the fire, with perhaps a few inadequate sentences. What they are thinking only the
novelist can tell us; and he does, to endless length.
But the dramatist finds it hard to control this
crowded traffic of our congested souls. Of course our
intellectual habits and interests may change. We may
weary of this fashion of counting every hair on our
characters' heads, and then sedulously splitting it.
The reign of the novel has been long and glorious.
Though Stendhal called for tragedy in prose, his own
answer was *Le Rouge et le Noir*; and *Wuthering
Heights* or *Tess of the D'Urbervilles* contains more
that is truly tragic than all the abortions of the
Victorian stage put together; but there are limits to
this ever-increasing magnification of the novelist's
microscope. And the necessities of the stage may
help to remind some writers of what is to-day too
easily forgotten, that art involves selection, and that
some things in life remain more important and
interesting than others; that it is the savage who

values alike glass bead and pearl, and that the happiest offspring are not bred of promiscuity. The drama, of its nature, cannot be as complex and complete as the novel; that need not, however, be an unmixed disadvantage. We might well have a reaction towards something simpler though not therefore less subtle, a kind of writing all the better as art for not being as exhaustive as a scientific treatise or a *procès verbal*. Further, the drama is learning to profit by simpler and saner staging; and we may realize from experiments like the Maddermarket Theatre at Norwich how much can be done not only by a return to an almost Elizabethan simplicity of scenery, but also—what is even more important—with actors unspoilt by the self-consciousness of the more educated classes, or the self-assertiveness of the professional stage. It seems incredible, indeed, that in any civilization at all like ours the drama should ever hold again that predominance among creative literature which it possessed under Pericles or Elizabeth; if Æschylus or Shakespeare lived to-day, it is difficult to imagine them writing only plays, if they wrote plays at all. But though hard pressed by the novel and by the ballet (as ancient tragedy under the Empire by the pantomime dancer), the drama remains precious. It began as a marvellous combination of many arts—music and song and dance and epic narrative; it has been shorn of these; but it survives for what it alone and no other art can do. Film and television offer new opportunities, often though these may be abused. Despite the protests of Goethe and Hazlitt and Lamb, made in an age when the theatre was at its basest, good drama *well* acted is better than read. The opposite view gives little credit to writers who certainly designed their work, not for the study, but the stage; it is a poor tribute to a cook to proclaim that her cakes make the most excellent mallets. Nothing can replace the serious drama. It is shy to flower, like the aloe; and quick, when it has flowered, to die again. Its great periods have come only half a dozen times in the history of Europe. But their masterpieces remain vividly alive; and this enduring life of tragedy remains one of the great consolations of the tragedies of life.

APPENDIX

SUMMARY OF THE *POETICS*

For reference, a general summary may help. It will be seen that Aristotle had a passion for classification; which has left his treatise as full of pigeon-holes as a dovecot. But the valuable part does not seem to me to lie in the pigeon-holes: it lies rather in the sudden glimpses of insight, the curt, but far-reaching dicta thrown out by the way. It is on those that this book has tried to concentrate.

I. 2. Poetry defined as *mimesis*, or "imitation" (*i.e* representation).

   3-5. Poetry, Dance, and Music classified according to Medium used:
     (*a*) Rhythm.
     (*b*) Melody.
     (*c*) Language.

   (Dancing=rhythm; Music=rhythm+melody; Verse=rhythm+language; Choral lyric= rhythm+melody+language.)

II. Subjects of imitative art:
     (*a*) Men finer than they are (*e.g.* tragedy).
     (*b*) Men meaner than they are (*e.g.* comedy).
     (*c*) Men as they are.

III. 1. Methods used by poetry:
     (*a*) Narrative.
     (*b*) Acting.

IV. 1-6. Poetry, Origins:
        (1) Human instinct for imitation.
        (2) Human instinct for rhythm and melody.

    7-10. Poetry, Development: Imitation of—
        (1) the fine→Epic→Tragedy
        (2) the mean→Satire→Comedy.

    12-14. Tragedy, Development:
        (1) The Dithyramb.
        (2) Aeschylus (second actor, less chorus, more dialogue).
        (3) Sophocles (third actor, scene-painting).

V. 1-3. Comedy, its Nature and Development: it deals with what is faulty or ugly, but not painful or destructive.

    4-5. Epic and Tragedy compared.
        (1) Likenesses:
           (a) Both metrical.
           (b) Both idealized.
        (2) Unlikenesses:

	Epic.	*Tragedy.*
(a)	One metre.	Many.
(b)	Covers many days.	Covers one.

VI. Tragedy, Definition.
        (1) Subject—an action (a) serious, (b) complete, (c) long enough.
        (2) Medium—language (beautified in various ways).
        (3) Method—acted, not narrated.
        (4) End—emotional relief (*catharsis*).

6-19. Tragedy, its Six Elements, in order of importance—Plot, Character, Thought, Language,
Music, Spectacle (which "concerns the
property-man rather than the poet").

VII. Plot, Structure of.

It must be:

(1) A complete whole, with Beginning, Middle,
and End; *i.e.* a logical unity.

(2) Of a size to be seen as a whole; *i.e.* a visible
unity—not too minute, nor yet too vast "as
if it were a creature a thousand miles long".

VIII. Plot, Unity of.

Not the same as Unity of Hero: it needs Unity of
Action.

IX. Plot, Subject of.

(1) Ideal truth—"poetry is more philosophical"
(*i.e.* more universal) "than history."

(2) But Tragedy generally keeps to figures from
traditional legend.

Plot, Kinds of.

(1) Worst—episodic (*i.e.* full of episodes not
causally connected).

(2) Best—surprise+seeming design, *i.e.* the Irony
of Fate.

X. Plots, Classification of.

(1) Simple, *i.e.* without Peripeteia or Discovery.

(2) Complex, *i.e.* with Peripeteia or Discovery.

XI. Plot, Elements of.

    (1) Peripeteia, *i.e.* when action meant to produce result *x* produces the opposite of *x*.

    (2) Discovery, *i.e.* recognition of persons, things, or facts.

    (3) Catastrophe, of tragic suffering.

XII. Subdivisions of tragic drama. Perhaps an interpolation.

XIII. Ideal Plot.

    (1) Complex.

    (2) Exciting pity and fear. It should therefore represent—

    Not (*a*) a good man coming to a bad end (this is shocking);

    nor (*b*) a bad man coming to a good end (neither moving, nor moral);

    nor (*c*) a very bad man coming to a bad end (moral, but not moving);

    but (*d*) a rather good man coming to a bad end.

The unhappy ending (*d*) therefore best, though not most popular. "Euripides is the most tragic of the poets."

XIV. Plot, Production of Pity and Fear by.

    1. Scenic effects are an inferior method.

    4. The Action may be:

        (1) of friend against friend;

    or (2) of enemy against enemy;

    or (3) of neutral against neutral.

    (1) is the most tragic.

6. The Action may be:

    (1) performed,
        (*a*) with full knowledge;
    or (*b*) in ignorance;

  or (2) intended, but *not* performed,
        (*a*) with full knowledge;
    or (*b*) in ignorance.

2(*b*) is best; then 1(*b*); then 1(*a*); then 2(*a*). (But contrast XIII above.)

XV. Character.

This should be:

    (1) good or fine;
    (2) true to type (*e.g.* unlike Melanippe);
    (3) true to human nature;
    (4) true to itself, consistent (*e.g.* unlike Iphigeneia);
    (5) probable, and logically constructed;
    (6) idealized.

XVI. Recognition or Discovery.

This may be:

    (1) by tokens—
        (*a*) congenital (birthmarks etc.);
        (*b*) acquired—(i) scars etc.; (ii) trinkets etc.

It may also be brought about:

    (2) by arbitrary self-revelation;
    (3) by emotional effect of associations;
    (4) by logical inference;
    (5) by illogical inference;
    (6) as a natural result of the situation (as in Sophocles, *Œdipus*).

(6) is best, then (4).

XVII. Composition, Rules for.
    (1) Conception:
        (*a*) Visualize events described.[1]
        (*b*) Act them with gestures.
    Importance of imaginative emotion. "Hence poetry requires genius *or* madness." (Cf. the contrast between Classic and Romantic, Apollonian and Dionysiac.)
    (2) Execution:
        (*a*) Outline.
        (*b*) Fill in details and episodes.

XVIII. (A later addition?)
    1. Plot, Structure of. Complication—Dénouement.
    2. Plot, Another Classification of (*cf.* X), as Simple or Complex, Tragedies of Moral Character or Tragedies of Passion.
    7. Choric utterances should be relevant (as in Sophocles, not in Euripides).

XIX. 1-3. Thought and Ideas in Tragedy.
    4. Diction in Tragedy.

[XX. Grammar.]

XXI. Diction (cont.). Kinds of words:
    (1) Current terms. (2) Foreign or dialect (*e.g.* "ennui"). (3) Metaphorical (*e.g.* "cold-blooded"). (4) Ornamental (*e.g.* "Sol"). (5) Coined (*e.g.* "Jabberwock"). (6) Modified: (*a*) lengthened (*e.g.* "faery"); (*b*) shortened (*e.g.* "sovranty"); (*c*) varied (*e.g.* "corse").

[1] A good example in Gosse and Archer's version of *The Master Builder*, where Hilda Wangel describes seeing Solness high on Lysanger tower, "as large as life". High on a tower, he would look tiny; not "large". Ibsen wrote "lyslevende"—"in living reality". The translators failed to visualize.

XXII. 1. Best Style.

    (1) Clear, but not mean.
    (2) Lofty, but not obscure.

  8. A certain Aríphrades, anticipating Wordsworth's objections to poetic diction, is curtly dismissed.

  9. "Much the greatest thing is mastery of metaphor."

10. Compound terms best for dithyramb (cf. our "ode").

Rare terms best for epic.

Metaphorical terms best for tragedy.

XXIII. Epic.

  1. It has unity of metre: it should have unity of action, like a dramatic plot.

  3. The superiority of Homer in unity of action.

XXIV. 1. Epic, Kinds of.

    Simple or Complex; Epics of Moral Character or Epics of Passion.

  5. Its metre, proved by experience, is the hexameter.

  7. Its need of impersonality. Homer's superiority in speaking largely through his characters.[1]

8-10. Its use of the marvellous. "Plausible impossibilities are better than unplausible possibilities" (*e.g.* Caliban than Sir Charles Grandison).

---

[1] Half the *Iliad*, it is said, consists of speeches—so close was epic already to drama. (Cf. the superiority of Boswell's *Johnson* to most biographies for the same reason.)

XXV. Theory of Criticism.

6-8. Improbabilities can be justified as (1) ideally true,[1] or (2) true to tradition,[2] or (3) true to actual fact, or (4) poetically right.

9. Other critical difficulties.

20. Real faults: (1) the impossible, (2) the irrational, (3) the immoral, (4) the inconsistent, (5) the inartistic.

XXVI. Epic *v.* Tragedy.

Epic is *said* to be better because free from the vulgarity of acting.

Answer. Vulgarity is the fault of actors, not of tragedy. And Tragedy can also be read.

Tragedy *is* better, because—

(1) it has all the elements of Epic, + Music and Spectacle;

(2) it is vividly present to us;

(3) it is more concise and concentrated;

(4) it has more unity.

---

[1] So Sophocles said—" *I* depict men as they should be: Euripides, as they are ".

[2] Aristotle instances the stories of the gods, condemned by Xenóphanes as immoral. (Contrast Aristotle's calm over this with Plato's indignation.)